Hand·me·ups

*Recrafting kids' clothes
with easy techniques
and fun designs*

Lorine Mason

kp

KRAUSE PUBLICATIONS
CINCINNATI, OHIO

www.mycraftivity.com
Connect. Create. Explore.

systems without permission in writing from the publisher, except by a reviewer who may quote brief passages in a review. Published by Krause Publications, an imprint of F+W Media, Inc., 4700 East Galbraith Road, Cincinnati, Ohio, 45236. (800) 289-0963. First Edition.

www.fwmedia.com

14 13 12 11 10 5 4 3 2 1

DISTRIBUTED IN CANADA BY FRASER DIRECT
100 Armstrong Avenue
Georgetown, ON, Canada L7G 5S4
Tel: (905) 877-4411

DISTRIBUTED IN THE U.K. AND EUROPE BY DAVID & CHARLES
Brunel House, Newton Abbot, Devon, TQ12 4PU, England
Tel: (+44) 1626 323200, Fax: (+44) 1626 323319
Email: postmaster@davidandcharles.co.uk

DISTRIBUTED IN AUSTRALIA BY CAPRICORN LINK
P.O. Box 704, S. Windsor NSW, 2756 Australia
Tel: (02) 4577-3555

Library of Congress Cataloging in Publication Data
Mason, Lorine.
 Hand-me-ups : recrafting kids' clothes with easy techniques and fun designs / by Lorine Mason. -- 1st ed.
     p. cm.
 Includes index.
 ISBN-13: 978-1-4402-0243-8 (pbk. : alk. paper)
 ISBN-10: 1-4402-0243-5 (pbk. : alk. paper)
 1. Children's clothing. 2. Clothing and dress--Remaking. 3. Fancy work. I. Title.
 TT635.M387 2010
 646.4'06--dc22
                    2009041373

Editor: Julie Hollyday
Designer: Julie Barnett
Production coordinator: Greg Nock
Photographers: Christine Polomsky, Ric Deliontoni and Al Parrish

Metric Conversion Chart

TO CONVERT	TO	MULTIPLY BY
inches	centimeters	2.54
centimeters	inches	0.4
feet	centimeters	30.5
centimeters	feet	0.03
yards	meters	0.9
meters	yards	1.1

ABOUT THE AUTHOR

Lorine Mason is an author, project designer and regular columnist whose work has been featured in print, on the Web and on television. She works with a variety of art mediums and strives to create items others will be inspired to re-create, hopefully adding their own personal touch. Her creative career started in retail, weaving its way through management and education positions along the path. This experience, along with a goal to stay on top of trends in color and style, gives her current work the edge manufacturers, publishers and editors have come to expect.

DEDICATION

I dedicate this book to all the people in my life who have gently nudged me forward when all I wanted to do was fade into the background: people I met during my years in school, at my many jobs and along the path as my family moved across the country and then across a border. I am who I am in part because of our meeting, and for that I am grateful. To the neighbors who became friends and the friends who became family: Eileen, Tina, Cyndi, Ann and Barb, to name just a few of the many who have made a wonderful impact on my life.

ACKNOWLEDGMENTS

Hand-Me-Ups was made possible by the great folks at Krause Publications, and I would like to thank them. A special thank you goes to my editor, Julie Hollyday, and a great photographer, Christine Polomsky. My new favorite city is Cincinnati.

I would like to thank a number of wonderful companies for their support during the making of *Hand-Me-Ups* and have listed their names in the Resources section. You will recognize their products in the projects throughout the book.

Contents

Introduction

If you have kids, then you probably have "the pile." We all have the pile, consisting of a variety of clothing items that are either too small or too big, stained, ripped or completely out of fashion. Or so you might think.

Before you hand off or hand down those supposedly useless items, cast a creative eye over the pile one more time. Perhaps it is the pair of pants that is too short for Suzie or that perfectly intact T-shirt with the unexplainable, unremovable stain on the front that catches your eye. Sure, you say, I see them, but what can I do with them?

Turn them into Hand-Me-Ups! Revamping these items can not only stretch your clothing budget but also provide your child with wardrobe options packed with personality and fun.

Inspiration everywhere you look

I am creatively motivated to do most things in life. I am inspired by almost everything around me—the way things around me appear different depending on the amount of sunshine on a particular day; the vast array of colors that surround my everyday life; or even a simple conversation with a friend. I come up with some of my best ideas while plowing through yet another thirty-five minutes on the elliptical trainer at the gym.

Look for what makes you smile and, most importantly, leave time in your day to allow that inspiration to form concrete ideas. And don't forget to take a look at your most fabulous creation: your child! Get inspired by your child's favorite sport, flowers, outside activities and colors.

Next, write down your idea or sketch it out! I keep notebooks in my house, my car and my purse. I jot down an idea and sketch out the design. It doesn't look like much at first glance, but the possibilities that can come from these idea books are inspiring. Think of your future Hand-Me-Ups projects as pieces of art; instead of painting and embellishing a canvas, you'll work directly on a piece of clothing.

Make it work for you

Don't stop with the pile sitting at your house. Sometimes a Hand-Me-Ups idea comes from fulfilling a need. "My child needs pajamas; it is spring and all the winter pajamas are on the clearance racks." From that came the transformation of a winter long john–style pajama set for $3 into a summer set guaranteed to be a perfect fit (see page 75). I love thrift stores and find the most interesting items for incredibly low prices. The thought of rescuing the items from life in the local dump only adds fuel to my creativity. Perfect examples of repurposing an item are found in the projects featuring denim finds (see pages 36-57).

Match up your idea with a project, using this book as a guideline. The possibilities are endless. You can follow the easy-to-read directions that are accompanied by wonderful photos to create a Hand-Me-Ups project. Or choose to be inspired by the designs, considering them jumping-off points when creating your own one-of-a-kind design using a favorite technique or embellishment. Colors and patterns, whether man-made or inspired by nature, have influenced the designs in this book. Find your inspiration and let the artist within you create your version of Hand-Me-Ups.

The Construction Site

What is the difference between deconstruction, construction and reconstruction? The simple explanation is:

Deconstruction

Deconstruction is the process of taking apart a garment or altering the original shape. Examples of this would be to open a side seam or remove a waistband.

Construction

Construction is the process of adding something to the original garment. Examples of this would be to paint a design or sew buttons onto an already complete garment.

Reconstruction

Reconstruction is the process of re-creating an item using its original components along with the addition of embellishment items. An example of this would be the addition of a skirt sewn to the bottom of a pair of overalls that were previously trimmed.

In this chapter, you'll learn the basics for painting, sewing and embellishing your Hand-Me-Ups projects. The techniques you'll see here are referenced through the rest of the book, so get familiar with this information. You'll learn how to prepare an item for painting (page 15) and how to add buttons (page 32), as well as some basic embroidery stitches (page 34). Read on to find out how to start making one-of-a-kind clothing your child will love!

Tools and Materials

Like a painter who works with only one brand of paintbrush or a mechanic who prefers a particular style of wrench, the correct tool can be the key to your success. Many choices are available, and the prices can be quite alarming. Take a few minutes to read through these recommendations; they will help you choose some of the best tools.

Ripping, Cutting and Rotary Tools

The first item you will need to get started on Hand-Me-Ups is a good **seam ripper**. I like the newer ones with the ergonomic handles because it seems I rip out a lot of seams. However, even the less expensive ones will do the trick. There are many available, some with longer blades and some with fancy covers. All you need is one that feels comfortable in your hand.

Next on the list are **scissors**. You will need a pair of **sewing scissors**, a pair of **embroidery scissors** and some **paper scissors** to cut out the patterns. **Decorative-edge scissors**, such as pinking or scalloped-edge scissors, are fun but can be pricey, so consider them an optional tool. The sewing and embroidery scissors do not have to be the finest quality of scissors to get started. Many scissors sets out there will do the job just fine and for beginning sewers, perhaps this is the best way to go. Similar to a chef's

cutlery collection, a good pair of scissors can make a difference; therefore price and quality are both things to consider when purchasing your first pair of scissors.

Having a **rotary cutter, cutting mat and ruler** are optional, but after you have experienced making quick, straight cuts without all the measuring and marking necessary when using scissors, you will be sold. The three items—rotary cutter, cutting mat and ruler—are really a set, because it would be difficult to use one without the others. Look for sales and complete sets for the best deals. I would suggest a mat no smaller than 18" × 24" (46cm × 61cm) as a good starting point.

Sewing Machines, Needles and Thread

To create Hand-Me-Ups, you will need a **basic sewing machine** to get started. If you own one with fancy embroidery stitches and have access to a serger that is great, but not necessary. Your sewing machine should have the ability to do a **straight stitch** and a **zigzag stitch**. You will need the zigzag stitch to finish the exposed seams.

Generally, **size 12/80** to **14/90 needles** will get you through all the projects in the book. Remember to change the needle once in a while; skipped stitches, breaking threads and uneven stitches are all clues you need to change the needle.

Thread is a hot topic among sewers and quilters. I use a name-brand polyester thread; beware of cheap thread because it can cause endless problems.

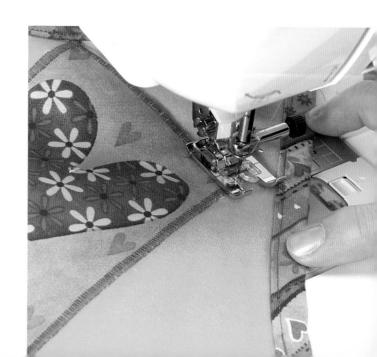

Paint, Brushes and Accessories

Your local craft and sewing stores sell a wide range of **fabric paints**. I use DecoArt's fabric paint and brushes and like the results I achieve. The paint is available in a wide range of colors, it blends together well, and the coverage is great.

Brushes made for fabric painting are best because they are made using stiffer bristles, which are needed to work the paint into the fibers of the fabric. A basic set consisting of No. 0 Liner, No. 5 Round and No. 4 Shader is perfect. I used inexpensive **1" (3cm) sponge brushes** to paint the background areas on most of the garments.

The **standard 1" (3cm) masking tape** is very useful to block off areas where you do not want paint to spread.

Graphite paper is used to transfer your patterns to the garments.

Other helpful items that should be in your work area are a **container filled with water** to wash your brushes, **paper plates** for your paint and lots of **paper towels** and **newsprint** to block off your work area.

Buttons, Ribbons, Embroidery Threads and Fun Embellishment Items

While you are browsing through your local thrift store or yard sale, look for **embellishment** possibilities.

Purchasing items just to use their embellishments is not unheard of, so keep that in mind when considering an item's overall price. The **pockets** or **tabs** from a pair of denim overalls and the **rickrack** from a curtain panel are embellishments up for grabs; all you need is the mind-set. The main consideration after the excitement of your find should be whether the items are washable and colorfast.

Look for **grab bags of ribbon and trim pieces** at fabric stores. Good deals are around; you just have to be aware of them.

I usually purchase **embroidery cotton** from the local craft store, and focus on the color more than the type. You will also need a good **embroidery needle** and an idea. Then you are ready to create!

Techniques

Everyday clothing and accessory items can be transformed using a bevy of clever techniques. Follow the step-by-step instructions to achieve a can-do attitude and experience the joy of making the projects in this book your own. Creating Hand-Me-Ups is truly an inexpensive way to expand your child's wardrobe, requiring from you only the most basic of crafting skills to achieve success.

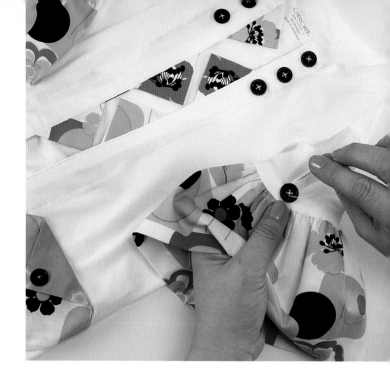

Getting Started with Fit

When purchasing items from a thrift or retail store, purchase a size that fits the intended wearer. When determining the intended wearer's measurements, follow the directions below to achieve the correct number.

Chest Measurement: Wrap the measuring tape over the fullest part of the chest, under the arms and straight across the back.

Waist Measurement: Wrap the measuring tape snugly around the natural waistline.

Hip Measurement: Wrap the measuring tape around the fullest part of the hips, parallel to the ground.

Finished Garment Length: Have the intended wearer try on the garment and measure either up from the ground to mark the hemline or down from the bottom edge of the upper part of the garment. These measurements are helpful in re-creating fashions from thrift stores or other purchased garments.

Garment Care and Handling

Before starting a project, I wash and then press thrift store purchases using the same method that I would after completion. If the item is not intended to be thrown into the washing machine, you are free to start on the project immediately. If you have concerns about fitting due to fabric shrinkage or are worried about colors running, take the time to prewash and press all items before beginning your design.

Read labels when purchasing trims, buttons, fabric paint and accessories. The most delicate button or trim just might transform a basic machine-washable item into a hand-wash-only design. The general rule is that the most delicate item

in your design will dictate the care required to maintain your garment, unless that item is removable. The decision is yours; just know what to look for when purchasing items for your designs. Follow the manufacturer's directions carefully to set the paint and inks, making them machine washable.

I love personal labels and thought it might be nice to give you the opportunity to create one for your Hand-Me-Ups projects. Feel free to copy the design (see the CD for the pattern) onto printable fabric on a copy machine or computer scanner, or trace and paint the design directly onto your garment.

Creating and Transferring a Pattern

What you create a pattern from is truly a personal choice. If you choose to create garments using the patterns provided with the book (see the CD), adjusting the size is simple. If you create your own, you can create some truly unique fashions. Wherever your pattern comes from, transferring it is easy, too!

Note

Please remember that there are copyright rules to follow when making items you will sell. In the case of the images and patterns provided in this book, feel free to adjust and use them for your personal use.

Creating your own pattern

If you want to create an image of your choice, this may be done a number of ways.

materials

Pattern • Pencil • Paper • Graphite paper

1 **Trace image**
Choose an image. Layer the tracing paper over the image. Using the pencil, trace the image onto the tracing paper.

2 **Draw freehand image**
If you are able, you can draw the image freehand using a pencil and a piece of paper.

·-<·-<·-<·-<·-<·❁ **TIP** ❁·>·->·->·->·->·-

*Tracing a pattern works best
with a simple, high-contrast image.*

Changing the size of a provided pattern

Here are two of the easiest materials I use to change the size of the provided patterns.

materials
Pattern CD • **Copy machine or Computer** • **Paper**

1 **Adjust size using copy machine**
Insert the CD into the CD-rom drive of your computer. Select the desired image from the CD. From your computer, print the image onto a piece of copy paper. Place the image into the copy machine, and adjust the image size up or down until you have the desired size. Make a copy of the adjusted image.

2 **Adjust size using image-editing program**
Insert the CD into the CD-rom drive of your computer. Select the desired image from the CD. Open the image in your favorite image-editing program. Adjust the size of the image as desired. Print the adjusted image onto printer paper.

Transferring a pattern

You have the pattern, and the next step is to transfer it to the garment or other item of your choice. This can be accomplished in a number of ways, but for the purposes of these projects I'll show you the simplest, and my favorite, method.

materials
Desired pattern • **Pencil or stylus** • **Graphite paper**

1 **Layer supplies**
Lay the graphite paper onto the garment in the area you want to transfer the pattern. Lay the pattern on top of the graphite paper. Using the pencil or stylus, trace the image. Lift the corner of the graphite paper to check the transfer.

More Ways to Transfer Patterns
Create a stencil *by cutting out the image (or pieces of the image) and adhering it to a piece of cardboard. Cut the cardboard shapes out with a pair of scissors. Use a pencil or disappearing fabric maker to trace the image onto the garment. I like to use this method when I know I'll be using the pattern a lot, for example when I want to create matching hats for a group of children. If you're feeling ambitious, you can simply **freehand draw** a design directly onto the garment using a pencil or fabric marker. I like doing this for free-form curly-cues and squiggle lines to fill in a design.*

Painting on Fabric

An artful makeover of a piece of clothing by painting fabric can be as simple as coloring in a coloring book. All you have to do is follow these simple instructions and remember that coloring outside the lines is still acceptable. It's artistic to adapt those little mistakes into design elements within your work.

Here, I'm using a piece of scrap denim to demonstrate this technique. Don't be afraid to cut up an old clothing item to practice on; you'll have more confidence when you embellish the intended item.

materials

Desired garment	Paper plate
Newsprint	Sponge brush
Paper towels	Fabric paint-brushes in a variety of sizes
Masking tape	
Bowl of water	Fabric paint marker
Fabric paint	

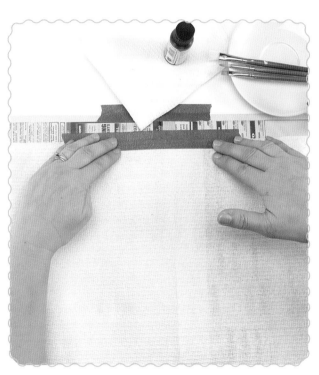

1 Prepare garment and work surface

Prepare the garment (see Garment Care and Handling on page 12).

Choose a working surface that is firm, even and large enough to fit the garment and your supplies. Cover the work area with a layer of newsprint, then a layer of paper towels. Using the masking tape, secure the paper layers to the surface. Have additional paper towels handy as well as the bowl of water to rinse the brushes as needed.

2 Paint first layer

Using the masking tape, cover any areas you do not want to paint.

Squeeze a silver dollar-size dollop of paint onto the paper plate. Using the sponge brush, paint the garment using smooth, even strokes. Work the paint into the fabric. Let the paint dry thoroughly. Paint additional coats as needed for an opaque look, allowing the paint to dry between each coat.

TIP

Run the edge of a ruler or a straight-edged item over the tape to assure proper adhesion.

3 Transfer pattern

Transfer the desired pattern (see Creating and Transferring a Pattern on page 13), making sure the pattern is in the desired area in the painted section.

4 Paint image base

Paint the design using the variety of brush sizes available. When painting, leave a thin, unpainted space between the design elements, such as between petals. (This spacing helps when adding highlighted lines in the next step of the design.)

Rinse the brushes in the bowl of water as needed.

· ‹ · ‹ · ‹ · ‹ · ‹ · ‹ ✿ T I P ✿ › · › · › · › · › · › · ›

Stroking in another color while the base color of paint is wet adds wonderful interest to the item.

· ‹ · ‹ · ‹ · ‹ · ‹ · ‹ ✿ T I P ✿ › · › · › · › · › · › · ›

The paint and fabric marker ink should be set when completely dry. Follow the manufacturer's directions carefully to achieve a washable garment. Washing the garment inside out in cold water is always a good idea.

5 Paint highlights and outline

Allow the image base to dry. Add highlight strokes in white and black line work around the designs. This can be accomplished using a liner brush and paint or a fabric marker. Let the paint or marker ink dry thoroughly.

If desired, repeat steps 1–5 on another area of the garment.

Bias Tape

Creating your own bias tape opens up so many design options. Bias tape allows you to finish raw edges and add a pop of color to a design. After you have tried it, you will find it hard to go back to plain purchased bias tape. (I find I only purchase narrow, double-fold bias tape now.)

I love to use a bias tape maker when pressing the strips. It makes things so easy. Creating bias strips of different widths is simple. Cut strips at a variety of widths. Purchase a bias tape maker in the appropriate size. Here is how you, too, can become addicted to designer bias tape.

materials

½ yard (½m) fabric	Iron
Cutting mat	Bias tape maker
Ruler	Scissors
Rotary cutter	
Straight pins	
Sewing machine	

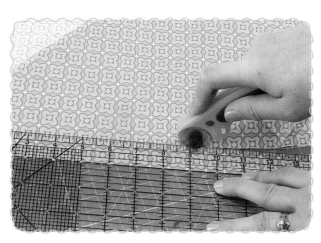

1 Cut first strip
Fold the fabric at a 45-degree angle and place it on top of the cutting mat, aligning the straight edges. Align the ruler 1" (3cm) away from the folded edge. Use the rotary cutter to cut the first strip.

2 Cut remaining strips
The first strip is cut at 1" (3cm) because you are cutting it along the fold, creating a 2" (5cm) wide strip when it is opened. Align the ruler 2" (5cm) from the fabric edge and cut the remaining strips 2" (5cm) wide.

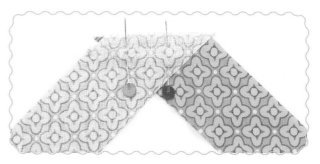

3 Pin strips
To achieve a continuous strip, lay the strips right sides together, overlapping them ¼" (6mm). Use straight pins to secure them.

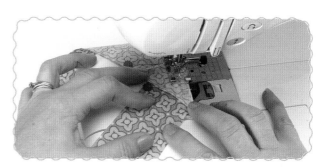

4 Sew strips
Stitch the strips together using a ¼" (6mm) seam.

5 Press seam open
Using the iron on a cotton setting, press the seam open.

17

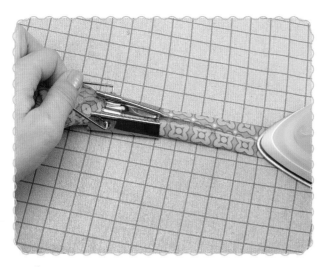

6 Thread through bias tape maker

Following the manufacturer's directions, feed the strip through the bias tape maker. Using the iron, press both edges in toward the middle of the strip.

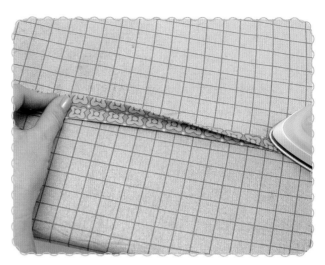

7 Press folded strip

Fold the strip in half and press well.
The bias tape is now ready to use on your projects.

Ties

Don't have a belt to go with that outfit? Take a couple of minutes and create one with a strip of fabric and one straight seam. Turn it right side out and press. Viola, a belt! This can also work to make a simple hair tie when using a shorter and wider piece of fabric.

materials

½ yard (½m) fabric   Safety pin

Sewing machine   Scissors

Iron

1 Prepare tie fabric

Cut two strips of fabric 1¼" (3cm) wide by the length of the fabric using your favorite cutting method. Turn each of the strips in half lengthwise, right sides together. Using the sewing machine, sew along the open edge the entire length of the strip with a ¼" (6mm) seam allowance.

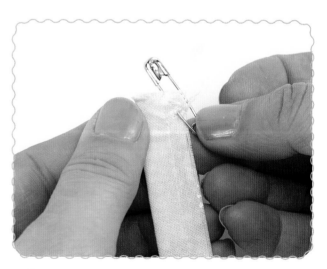

2 Secure safety pin

Hook the safety pin on the end of the stitched fabric.

3 Insert pin head
Push the safety pin headfirst into the fabric. Work the pin through the strip.

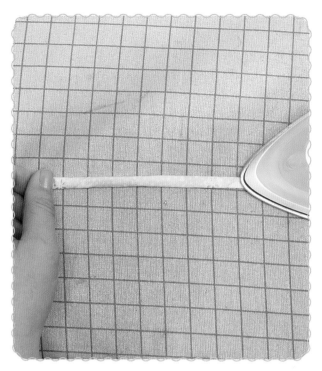

5 Iron tie
Using the iron, press the fabric tube.

4 Pull pin through fabric
Pull the pin out the other end of the tie so the fabric is right side out.

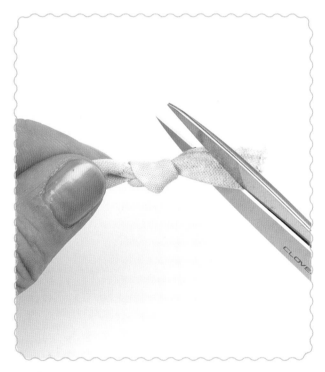

6 Finish ends
Tie each end with an overhand knot. Trim the ends at an angle.

Finishing a Raw Edge

If you have a loose thread someone is likely to come along and pull it. Let's fix that before it becomes an issue with a fast way to finish off those freshly cut seams. Don't have a serger or fancy overcast stitch on your sewing machine? No worries. Simply use a zigzag stitch on your machine and take control of those fraying edges in no time at all. This technique can be used after joining seams and to finish a garment.

materials

Sewing machine

Iron

Finishing a raw edge after joining seams

Here, I'm using the overcast stitch,
but a zigzag stitch works just as well.

Finishing a raw edge after finishing the garment

If you think your garment could use some extra reinforcements,
finish the edges of all the seams. Here, I'm using the zigzag stitch.

1 Finish raw edge
After joining two pieces of fabric, use the iron to press the seam flat together (not open, as is usual). Using the overcast or zigzag stitch on the sewing machine, sew along the raw edges to sew the fabric flaps together.

Ruffles

What says girly more than ruffles? Remember twirling and dancing about just to see how far that skirt could extend in full swing when you were a child? Not much has changed, and ruffles are not difficult to create. Trust me.

materials

Fabric strips (see projects for specific yardages)

Scissors

Straight pins

Sewing machine

Iron

1 Prepare fabric
Cut the fabric strips according to the instructions provided with each garment to determine the exact width needed for a particular design. Pin the strips right sides together along the short ends.

2 Join fabric
Join the strips, sewing the short ends together with a ¼" (6mm) seam allowance.

Folded or Single Layer Ruffle

Depending on the garment, you may want to use a folded ruffle that has a neat finished edge (seen in step 3), or a single layer ruffle that allows a little fraying (seen in step 4).

If a folded ruffle is not required, simply join the strips together and proceed to sewing gathering stitches in step 4.

Whichever you choose, the ruffles are sure to be cute!

4 **Pull gathering threads**
Layer the garment and the ruffle right sides together. Adjust gathers by pulling the bobbin (under treads) thread and distributing the gathers evenly along the garment.

3 **Finish seam and place gathering stitches**
Finish the raw edges of the joining seam (see Finishing a Raw Edge on page 20). Fold the ruffle in half lengthwise, right-sides out (see Folded or Single Layer Ruffle above). Using the iron, press the fabric.

Sew two rows of gathering stitches, ⅜" (1cm) and ¼" (6mm) from the raw edges along the top edge (the long edge) of the ruffle.

5 **Secure ruffle to fabric**
Pin as needed to secure the ruffle to the garment piece.

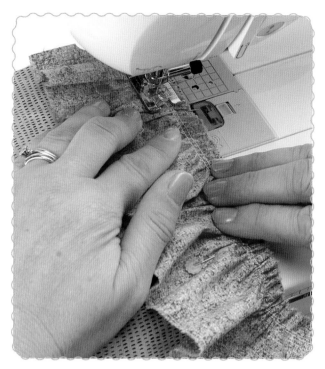

6 Stitch ruffle
Stitch the ruffle to the fabric using a ½" (1cm) seam.

8 Finish raw edges
Fold the ruffle up again to expose the seam edge. Finish the raw edges.

7 Press garment
Using the iron, press the ruffle away from the garment edge.

Pleats

A little more formal than ruffles but still fun, pleats add a touch of controlled spontaneity to a skirt. Pleats can be lined up straight and stitched neatly into a waistband of a skirt, or they can be left open to a free flowing fullness along the hemline. Here, I show you how to add a pleat to a hem.

materials

Fabric strips (see projects for specific yardages)	**Measuring tape or Cutting mat**
Scissors	**Fabric marker**
Sewing machine	**Straight pins**
Iron	

1 Join fabric
Cut the fabric strips according to the instructions provided with each garment. Join the strips, right sides together, by sewing the short ends with a ¼" (6mm) seam allowance. Finish the raw edges of the joined seam (see Finishing a Raw Edge on page 20).

2 Mark pleats
With the fabric right side up, line the top edges of the fabric along the markings of a cutting mat or measuring tape. Using a fabric marker, mark the fabric, spacing marks 1" (3cm) apart.

⸱⸱⸱ TIP ⸱⸱⸱

Use the cutting mat or measuring tape to line up the marks and start the folds.

3 Fold first pleat

Starting with the second 1" (3cm) mark, fold the second and fourth marking in toward the third mark, creating an inverted pleat.

4 Fold second pleat

Pin to secure the pleat. Repeat, folding the fifth and seventh marks in toward the sixth mark. Use straight pins to secure the fold.

5 Continue pleating

Continue folding and pinning until you reach the end of the fabric.

6 Sew pleat and fabric together

Lightly press the top of the pleats. With the right sides together, pin the pleated strip to the garment. Stitch them together using a ½" (1cm) seam. Finish the seams.

7 Press pleat

Using the iron, press the pleated strip down from the garment.

Yo-Yos

Using circles of fabric and a row of gathering stitches sewn with needle and thread, you can create in minutes a sweet embellishment perfect for all kinds of garments. Match the fabrics perfectly or add a punch of color with a contrasting fabric yo-yo.

materials

Fabric	Needle
Yo-yo maker	Thread
Scissors	Pom-pom (optional)

1 Assemble Yo-yo
Lay the fabric right side down on top of the yo-yo base plate. Center the disk on top of the plate, aligning the holes. Snap the disk into the plate.

3 Begin sewing
Thread the needle. Knot the end of the thread to secure it.
Turn the raw edge of the fabric in toward the center of the disk, holding it in place with your fingers. Insert the needle into the starting point from the disk side.

2 Trim fabric
Using the scissors, trim the fabric, leaving a ¼" (6mm) border.

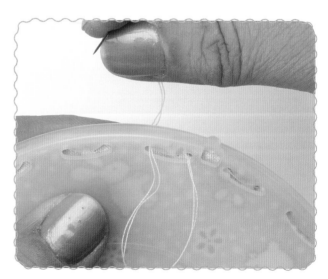

4 Continue sewing
Sewing only through the open spaces of the disk, continue sewing around the disk, ending in the same hole as you began.

5 Gather fabric

Remove the disk from the plate. Pinch the seam at the edge with your fingers and remove the fabric from the disk. Pull the thread, gathering the yo-yo while folding the seam inward.

7 Optional: Add pom-pom

Sew through the center of the yo-yo, adding a pom-pom to the other side of the fabric. Knot the thread to secure the pom-pom.

6 Secure gathers

Adjust the gathers as needed. Using the needle and thread, stitch around the opening. When you are satisfied the yo-yo will not come undone, knot the thread to secure it.

8 Attach yo-yo to garment

Stitch the completed yo-yo to your garment. If using a pom-pom, attach the yo-yo so the pom-pom faces out.

Prairie Points

Prairie points is a quilting technique that has been around for ages. You can achieve great success the first time out because this quick technique takes only the most basic folding and pressing skills.

materials

Fabric (see projects for specific measurements)

Scissors

Iron

Straight pins

Sewing machine

Ruler

Rotary cutter

Cutting mat

1 Prepare fabric
Cut squares from the fabric (measurements are given in specific projects). Fold one fabric square in half, right sides out. Press the crease with the iron.

2 Iron fabric
Fold the square from corner to corner. Press lightly with the iron to keep the folds crisp.

3 Arrange prairie points

Arrange the prairie points in a row with the open edges of the squares along one side. Tuck the squares into the openings, adjusting the spacing to fit the garment or bag. Pin as needed to secure.

5 Trim excess fabric

Trim the excess fabric from the top of the prairie points ¼" (6mm) above the stitching line.

The prairie points are now ready to use as directed in the projects.

4 Stitch prairie points

Stitch ¼" (6mm) above the center line of the prairie point.

Appliqué

If you can trace a pattern, cut along the lines and iron the designs onto your garment you can do an Appliqué. Any stitching that is done is up to you—add as much or as little as you choose.

materials

Pattern	Iron
Fusible web	Scissors
Fabric	Sewing machine

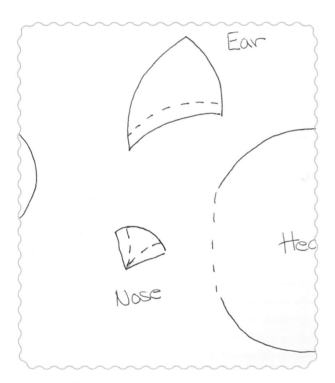

1 Transfer pattern
Trace or draw the design onto the paper liner of the fusible web (see Creating and Transferring a Pattern on page 13). Add seam lines (the dash lines in this photo) to each piece so there is no gap when layering them.

2 Prepare fabric
Remove the opposite side of the paper liner from the fusible web. Using the iron, press the fusible web to the wrong side of the fabric (read the manufacturer's instructions to determine the proper heat setting).

3 Cut out design
Using the scissors, cut out the design.

4 Fuse to garment
Remove the paper backing of the fusible web and arrange the fabric pieces onto the garment. Using the iron on a cotton setting, press the fabric pieces well.

5 Topstitch design
Topstitch through the appliqué and garment front along the inside edges of the appliqué. Do not worry about perfection; loosely following the lines provides additional interest in the design.

Adding Buttons

When choosing buttons for your project, the buttons' size, color, weight and washability, are all things you should consider. Whether using thread in a color that matches the button perfectly, or one that is a contrasting bright or complementary color, be sure it is a good quality and strong thread. Embroidery thread is a nice choice and is available in wonderful colors.

There are other things to be aware of when creating designs using buttons. Buttons can add substantial weight to the design, so choose carefully. When deciding just where to add buttons, make sure their placement is decorative but not bothersome to the wearer. Note: Be careful when adding buttons to young children's clothing because they can be a choking hazard.

materials

Pattern

Disappearing fabric marker

Cotton swab

Glue

Buttons

Needle

Thread

Scissors

1 Mark button placement
Using a provided pattern or by freehand drawing a design, mark the buttons' placement with the fabric marker.

2 Apply glue
Using the cotton swab, apply a small amount of glue to the underside of the button, being careful not to get glue in the holes.

3 Place button

Place the button in its designated spot on the pattern. Repeat steps 2 and 3 until you have placed all the buttons.

5 Complete stitch

Complete the stitch from one button to another by bringing the needle up through the closest hole in the following button. Repeat steps 4 and 5 to complete stitching the row of buttons.

4 Stitch buttons

To secure the buttons further and add decoration, use the needle and thread to stitch the buttons. Tie a knot at the end of the thread to secure it. Bring the needle up and through the holes in each button.

Running Stitch

This is the simplest of all embroidery stitches! The basic up-and-down motion of going in and out of the fabric is all there is to it. The length of the stitches is up to you and with practice can be controlled with little effort.

materials

Pattern

Disappearing
fabric marker

Embroidery thread

Scissors

Embroidery
needle

1 Apply design
Using the fabric marker, trace the pattern or draw a freehand design.

2 Stitch design
Cut a length of thread 24" (60cm) or less (longer amounts tend to knot or become tangled). Thread the needle and tie a knot at the end. Slide the needle in and out of the fabric, making evenly spaced stitches. The length of the stitch is your choice.

Backstitch with Beading

You have heard the expression, "Take one step forward and another back." This technique follows that saying while adding a bead. Before long you won't even be thinking about the next stitch, because it will fall into place naturally.

materials

Embroidery thread

Scissors

Embroidery needle

Beads

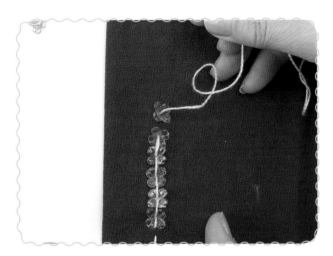

1 Begin stitch
Cut a length of thread 24" (60cm) or less (longer amounts tend to knot or become tangled). Thread the needle and tie a knot at the end. Slide the needle into the fabric and make one running stitch (see page 34), coming back up through the top of the garment.

2 Add bead
Add a bead and make another stitch into the garment.

3 Stitch backward
Come back up through the center of the bead, stitching backward.

4 Add new bead
Add a bead and make another stitch forward. Repeat steps 1–4 until you've added the desired amount of beads.

- - - - - - - - - - - TIP - - - - - - - - - -

Want to make sure you did this right?
Flip the garment inside-out. There should be
a space between each of the stitches.

Denim Do-Overs

Denim is tough. It rarely wears out and is usually set aside due to a size or style change. The techniques you learned in Chapter 1 can be applied to update any denim piece.

Check out the *Painted Pansy Jean Jacket* (page 38) and the *Patchwork Overalls* (page 42) for some painted creations with or without a pattern. The *Cropped Floral Jeans With Tie Belt* (page 47) and *Jump for Joy* (page 51) demonstrate how easy it is to alter denim clothes for the perfect fit. Check out the *All-Buttoned-Up Vest* (page 56) for a simple way to update a dated denim piece.

It's time to pull out that denim from the back of your closet or pick up an inexpensive piece from your local thrift store or yard sale and get ready for some fun.

Painted Pansy Jean Jacket

Painting fabric never seemed so simple. A denim jacket becomes the perfect canvas for your painting. No skills needed—just a little patience and some masking tape, and you are on your way to becoming a true fashion crafter.

materials

Denim jacket

Fabric paint in white, black and periwinkle

Paintbrushes in No. 0 liner, No. 5 round and No. 4 shader

Bowl with water

Materials for the following Techniques
- Garment Care and Handling (page 12)
- Creating and Transferring a Pattern (page 13)
- Painting on Fabric (page 15)

1 Prepare and paint jacket

Prepare the garment for use (see Garment Care and Handling on page 12). Prepare the jacket for painting (see Painting on Fabric on page 15). Tape the jacket to the surface to prevent movement.

Squeeze the periwinkle paint onto the paper plate. Using the sponge brush, paint the masked off areas of the jacket front. Let the paint dry thoroughly, and repeat for opaque coverage. Use the bowl with water as needed to rinse the brushes.

2 Paint pockets

Squeeze the white paint onto the paper plate. Using the No. 4 shader, paint the pocket flaps of the jacket. Let dry. Repeat as needed for opaque coverage.

3 Transfer and paint image

Transfer the pansy pattern (see the CD for the pattern) to the jacket front (see Creating and Transferring a Pattern on page 13).

Using the liner brush and black paint, outline the flowers following the pattern lines.

4 Add detail

Rinse the liner brush well. With the white paint, add highlights to the petals, using the project photo as a guide. Let the paint dry thoroughly.

5 Paint back of jacket

Repeat steps 1–4 to decorate the back of the jacket.

Follow the paint manufacturer's directions for laundering instructions.

Stained Glass Rose Jacket

Transforming the age-old art of stained glass into a painting on the back of a denim jacket is not as difficult as it would seem. By following the simple step-by-step instructions, even the most inexperienced painter can achieve the desired look.

materials

Denim jacket

Fabric paint in white, olive green, pink and black

Paintbrushes in No. 0 liner, No. 5 round and No. 4 shader

Materials for the following Techniques
- Getting Started with Fit (page 12)
- Garment Care and Handling (page 12)
- Creating and Transferring a Pattern (page 13)
- Painting on Fabric (page 15)

1 Prepare and paint

Prepare the garment for use (see Garment Care and Handling on page 12). Prepare the jacket for painting and paint it with the white paint (see Painting on Fabric on page 15). Let the paint dry thoroughly.

Transfer the Stained Glass Rose pattern (see the CD for the pattern) to the front and back of the jacket (see Creating and Transferring a Pattern on page 13).

Using the shader and round paintbrushes and pink and green paints, paint the rose and its leaves. Dipping the paintbrush into white paint, add and blend it through the wet paints to add additional dimension to the petals and leaves. Let the paints dry. Use the bowl with water to rinse the brushes as needed.

2 Add highlights

Using the white paint and the shader and round paintbrushes, add highlights to each petal and leaf.

3 Add outline

Using the black paint and the liner brush, outline the petals and leaves following the lines of the pattern.

4 Embellish design

Using the black paint and liner brush, embellish the design with curvy lines.

5 Paint jacket front

If desired, repeat steps 1–4 to add rose vines to the front pocket flaps.

Follow the manufacturer's instructions to set the paint.

⚬⚬⚬⚬⚬⚬⚬⚬ TIP ⚬⚬⚬⚬⚬⚬⚬⚬

*When adding the embellishments, you can use
a black fabric marker. Getting curvy lines may take
a bit of practice and a steady hand because
fabric markers are typically best for straight lines.
Practice on some scrap denim
to see if it will work for you.*

Patchwork Overalls

Simple geometric shapes and bright colors combine perfectly to create a fun overalls make-over suitable for children of all ages. Add the playful swirls and some outlining in jet black to make the colors really pop.

materials

Denim overalls

Fabric paint in green, yellow and black

Paintbrushes in No. 0 liner, No. 5 round and No. 4 shader

Black fabric marking pen

Ruler

Materials for the following Techniques
- Garment Care and Handling (page 12)
- Painting on Fabric (page 15)

1 Prepare and paint overalls

Prepare the garment for use (see Garment Care and Handling on page 12). Prepare the overalls for painting (see Painting on Fabric on page 15).

Squeeze the green and yellow paints onto the paper plate. Using the No. 4 shader, paint the masked-off areas of the overalls. Let the paint dry thoroughly and repeat for an opaque coverage.

2 Paint additional areas

Remove the masking tape. If desired, mask off other areas and repeat the painting process described in step 1.

3 Outline painted patches

When adding the design to the legs of the overalls, put a paper towel inside the leg at the section you want to paint. Follow steps 1 and 2 to paint the area as desired.

Remove any masking tape. Using the fabric marker and a ruler, outline the painted areas. Let the ink dry.

4 Embellish painted patches

Using the liner brush and black paint, add random swirls on top of the painted areas. (For interest, make some lines thicker than others.) If you prefer, you can draw the lines onto the painted surface using the fabric marker. Let the paint or ink dry thoroughly.

5 Decorate back of overalls

Repeat steps 1–4 to decorate the back side of the overalls. Follow the paint manufacturer's directions to set the paint.

Coming Up Daisies Vest

Sometimes we tire of wearing the same plain old thing. Improve one of your children's most basic of wardrobe items with a little paint and an idea. Stylized painted blossoms and black polka dots work together perfectly to upgrade this simple denim vest.

materials

Denim vest

Fabric paint in black, magenta, turquoise, white and yellow

Paintbrushes in No. 0 liner, No. 5 round and No. 4 shader

Bowl with water

Materials for the following Techniques
- Getting Started with Fit (page 12)
- Garment Care and Handling (page 12)
- Creating and Transferring a Pattern (page 13)
- Painting on Fabric (page 15)

1 Prepare and paint vest

Prepare the garment for use (see Garment Care and Handling on page 12). Using the white paint and sponge brush, paint the back of the vest (see Painting on Fabric on page 15). Let the paint dry thoroughly. Repeat for opaque coverage.

Transfer the flower pattern (see the CD for the pattern) randomly to the back of the vest (see Creating and Transferring a Pattern on page 13).

Note: The flowers overlap and run off the edges of the painted areas.

•‹•‹•‹•‹•‹•‹• ❀ **TIP** ❀ •›•›•›•›•›•›•

If your vest has a tab and you don't want to paint on it, tape it as I did here.

2 Paint flowers

Using the No. 5 round and No. 4 shader, paint the flowers using the yellow, pink and turquoise paints. Let the paint dry and repeat for an opaque coverage. Use the bowl of water to rinse the brush as needed.

3 Outline design

Using the liner brush and black paint, outline each of the petals. Let the paint dry thoroughly.

4 Add highlights

Rinse the brush well. Using white paint, add highlights to each petal. Let the paint dry thoroughly.

5 Embellish with dots

Add random dots to the center of each flower by dipping the back end of the liner brush into black, yellow and white paints. Apply black dots onto the white background. Let the paint dry.

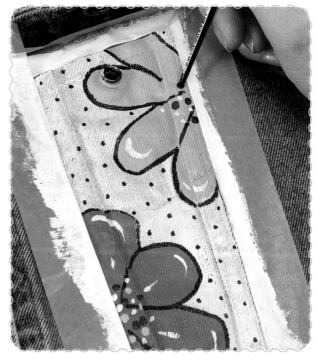

6 Decorate front of vest

Repeat steps 1–5 to decorate the vest front.
Follow the manufacturer's directions to set the paint.

Cropped Floral Jeans With Tie Belt

Many times our children grow taller without gaining a pound. It is called a growth spurt. Why not celebrate it with a trendy upgrade from too short jeans to fashion-forward capris and a matching tie belt?

materials

Too short jeans

Disappearing fabric marker

Rotary cutter

Cutting mat

Ruler

¼ yard (¼m) cotton or cotton-blend fabric

Buttons

Fabric paints in olive green, blue and black

Paintbrushes in No. 0 liner, No. 5 round and No. 4 shader

Straight pins

Bowl with water

Materials for the following Techniques:
- Getting Started with Fit (page 12)
- Garment Care and Handling (page 12)
- Creating and Transferring a Pattern (page 13)
- Painting on Fabric (page 15)
- Finishing a Raw Edge (page 20)
- Adding Buttons (page 32)

Deconstruction

1 Cut jean legs

Prepare the garment for use (see Garment Care and Handling on page 12). Have the intended wearer try the jeans on. Mark the desired finished length of the capris with the disappearing fabric marker.

Lay the jeans on top of the cutting mat. Using the ruler and the rotary cutter, find the mark and cut straight across the jean leg, completely removing the bottom of the leg. Measure up 2" (5cm) from the cut and trim straight across. (The additional 2" [5cm] allows for the cuff length.)

Reconstruction

2 Measure cuff

Measure the circumference of the bottom of the leg and add 1" (3cm) to this number. (In this case, I have a total of 15½" [39cm].)

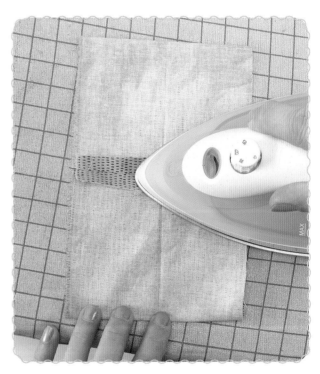

3 Cut and sew fabric

Using the measurement from step 2 as the length, cut a strip of fabric 5" (13cm) wide.

Fold the fabric strip right sides together and stitch the short end using a ½" (1cm) seam allowance. Press the seam open.

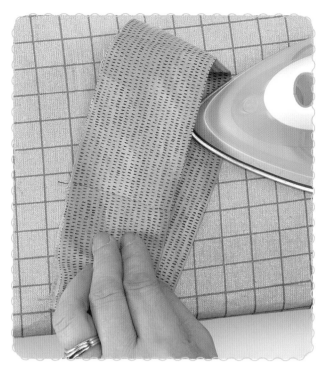

4 Press fabric
Fold the strip in half, so the right sides face out. Using the iron, press the fabric at the fold.

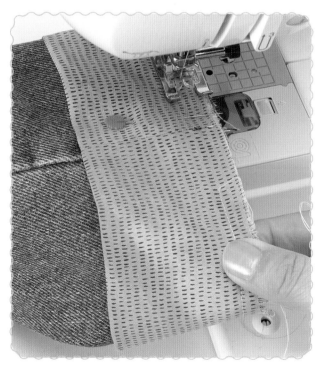

5 Attach fabric to jeans
Pin the rough edge of the fabric cuff to the bottom edge of the pant leg, matching the outside seam line of the jeans with the seam line of the cuff. Stitch using ½" (1cm) seams.

6 Embellish cuff
Finish the seam (see Finishing a Raw Edge on page 20). Use the iron to press the cuff down from the pant leg. Sew two buttons along the outside seam line of the cuff.
Repeat steps 2–6 for the other cuff.

7 Begin tie belt
Cut a strip of fabric 4½" × 45" (11cm × 114cm). Fold the strip in half lengthwise, right sides out, and press. Place the folded strip onto the cutting mat. Using the rotary cutter and the ruler, trim both ends of the fabric strip at a 45-degree angle.

8 Sew tie belt

Fold the fabric lengthwise, right sides together. Using the sewing machine, stitch a ¼" (6mm) seam allowance, leaving a 3" (8cm) opening. Turn the fabric strip right side out through the 3" (8cm) opening. Using the iron, press the fabric.

9 Finish belt

Top stitch the belt ¼" (6mm) away from all the edges. Thread the belt through the belt loops of the jeans and tie overhand knots at both ends of the belt.

Sew buttons to the center of each of the belt loops.

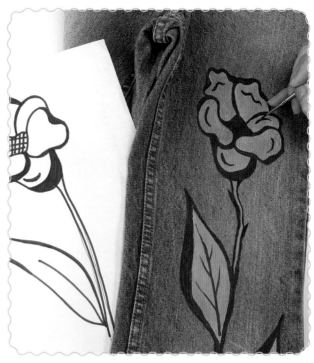

10 Paint jeans

Transfer the flower pattern (see the CD for the pattern) to the left pant leg of the jeans (see Creating and Transferring a Pattern on page 13).

Prepare the jeans for painting (see Painting on Fabric on page 15).

Squeeze equal amounts of light green and blue onto the paper plate and mix together. Using the No. 4 shader brush, paint the flower petals. Let the paint dry. Repeat for opaque coverage.

Squeeze the green paint onto the paper plate. Using the No. 4 shader brush, paint the stem and leaves. Let the paint dry. Repeat for opaque coverage.

Using the liner brush and black paint, outline the flower design, adding the flower center, petal creases, thorns to the stem and veins to the leaves. For interest, make some lines thicker than others. Note: If you prefer, draw the lines onto the dry painted surface prior to painting.

Follow the manufacturer's directions to set the paint.

TIP

I liked the idea of matching the color of the flower petals closely to the fabric I chose for the cuff and belt additions, so I mixed the blue and green used to paint the flower petals. You can do the same, or pick a single color—perhaps your little girl's favorite!

Jump for Joy

A jumper is a mainstay of every little girl's wardrobe, because it provides the versatility of year-round fashion. A simple short-sleeved T-shirt creates casual comfort and is perfect to wear on a warm summer day. Wearing a cozy turtle-neck or long-sleeved blouse provides the extra warmth needed for those cooler days come fall and winter.

materials

Denim overalls

Cutting mat

Ruler

Rotary cutter

Pen

Scissors (optional)

1 yard (1m) cotton or cotton-blend fabric

Iron

Straight pins

Sewing machine

Assorted buttons

Fabric paints

Paintbrushes in No. 0 liner, No. 5 round and No. 4 shader

Materials for the following Techniques
- Getting Started with Fit (page 12)
- Garment Care and Handling (page 12)
- Creating and Transferring a Pattern (page 13)
- Painting on Fabric (page 15)
- Ties (page 18)
- Finishing a Raw Edge (page 20)
- Pleats (page 24)

Deconstruction

1 Measure and mark

Prepare the overalls for use (see Garment Care and Handling on page 12). Place the overalls onto the cutting mat. Using the ruler and pen, place a mark 1" (3cm) below the natural waistline along each side seam of the overalls. Draw a line connecting the two marks.

3 Optional: Remove back pocket

If the overalls do not have a front pocket on the bib, you can create one by removing a pocket from the bottom portion of the jumper. Using the scissors, cut ½" (1cm) away from the sides and bottom edges of the pocket and 1" (3cm) across the top edge. Turn under ½" (1cm) along the top edge of the pocket and press well. Set aside.

· ‹ · ‹ · ‹ · ‹ · ‹ · ‹ · ❀   T I P   ❀ · › · › · › · › · › · › ·

In the project photo you see on page 51, I used decorative-edge scissors to cut off the pocket—it adds another touch of cute to the project!

2 Cut overalls

Using the rotary cutter, cut along this line, removing the bottom section of the jumper.

Reconstruction

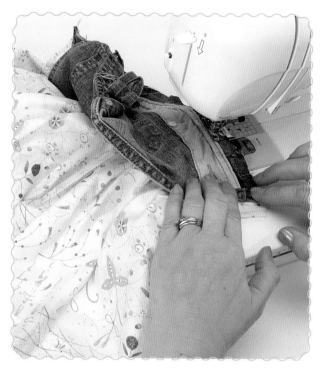

4 Determine skirt size

Review Getting Started with Fit on Page 12. To determine the length of the skirt, do the following:

With the child wearing the trimmed top portion of the overalls, measure down from the bottom edge of the denim top to the desired hemmed length of a skirt. Add 4½" (11cm) to this number to allow for the seams and the hem. Using the printed fabric, cut two pieces, the width of the fabric × the measurement calculated above.

Pleat both pieces of fabric (see Pleats on page 24). Lightly press the top of the pleats. Depending on the width of the denim top, it may be necessary to sew an additional length of fabric to each of the front and back skirt sections before pleating.

Measure along the front bottom edge of the overalls top from side seam to side seam. Add 1" (3cm) to this measurement. Cut the pleated width of fabric using this measurement, centering and/or adjusting the pleats, trimming excess fabric from one or both sides if necessary. Repeat for the back of the jumper.

5 Attaching skirt to overalls top with no side buttons

With right sides together, stitch the two fabric pieces together along the short edges. Press the seams open. Finish the seams (see Finishing a Raw Edge on page 20).

Pin the fabric skirt to the bottom edge of the overalls top, matching the side seams (if possible). Stitch using a ½" (1cm) seam.

6 If overalls do not have side button

Finish the seams (see Finishing a Raw Edge on page 20). Press the skirt down from the overalls top. Shown here are the seams on the inside of the garment when the skirt the pressed down.

7 If overalls had side button opening

If your overalls had a side button opening, the skirt pieces will be attached to the front and back sections separately. To do this, stitch the skirt front and back pieces together at the side seams leaving 2" (5cm) open at the top of each side seam. Press the seams open.

Pin the skirt panels to the front and back sections of the denim overalls top, matching the pressed side seams with the finished side openings on the overalls.

9 Press hem

Turn the bottom edge of the skirt under 2" (5cm) and press well. Turn under an additional 2" (5cm) and press again.

8 Attaching skirt to side button opening

Stitch the skirt to the overalls top. Finish the raw edges (see Finishing a Raw Edge on page 20). Press the skirt panels down form the jumper top.

10 Stitch hem

Using the sewing machine, stitch along the top edge of the hem. Press the hem well.

11 Make ties

Cut a 2" × 45" (5cm × 114cm) strip of fabric. Make a tie for the outfit (see Ties on page 18).

Fold the tie belt in half and mark the center point with a pin. Pin the center point of the belt to the center back of the jumper, positioning it just above the waist seam. Top stitch the belt in place.

If the jumper has side buttons (as I show here), use a needle and thread to hand stitch the tie in one spot on each side. If the jumper doesn't have side buttons, use the sewing machine or a needle and thread to stitch the tie in one spot on each side.

12 Optional: Adding a front pocket

If you don't have a bib pocket for the jumper, you can add one. Refer to step 3 to remove a back pocket.

To attach the pocket, pin it to the center front of the jumper top. Top stitch all the way around the edges of the pocket.

13 Embellish pocket

Choose a design element from the skirt fabric and copy the design onto a piece of tracing paper; then transfer the design to the front of the jumper pocket (see Creating and Transferring a Pattern on page 13).

Prepare the jumper for painting (see Painting on Fabric on page 15). Paint in the designs using fabric paints. Let the paint dry.

Follow the manufacturer's directions to set the paint.

All-Buttoned-Up Vest

Instead of running out the door to purchase something new for your child, consider creating something exciting from an item already hanging in her closet. Kick it up a notch with the addition of a few buttons and colorful stitching lines.

materials

Denim vest

Shell buttons in sizes ⅜" (9mm), ½" (1cm) and ¾" (2cm)

Navy blue embroidery thread

Red embroidery thread

Fabric marking pen

Ruler

Scissors

Materials for the following Techniques
- Garment Care and Handling (page 12)
- Creating and Transferring a Pattern (page 13)
- Adding Buttons (page 32)
- Running Stitch (page 34)

1 Lay out pattern

Prepare the garment for use (see Garment Care and Handling on page 12).

Lay the vest on a flat surface and position the buttons on the front of the vest in the desired pattern. A button layout guide has been provided (see the CD for the pattern) but consider changing up the design to custom fit your vest.

TIP

When you are stitching the buttons in step 2, starting at one side and working across the front of the vest in a continuous line works wonderfully.

2 Secure buttons

When you are happy with the layout, secure the buttons to the front of the vest using the navy blue embroidery thread (see Adding Buttons on page 32).

3 Design back of vest

Transfer the pattern of the bird to the back of the vest using the project photo as a guide to placement (see Creating and Transferring a Pattern on page 13). Using the fabric pen, freehand draw a curved line onto the back of the vest, being sure it curves under the bird's feet (this is a branch the bird is perched on). Lay buttons along the branch line. When you are happy with the layout, secure the buttons to the front of the vest as you did in step 2.

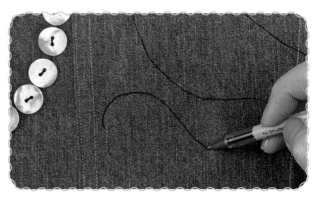

4 Embroider bird

Using the embroidery needle and an 18" (46cm) length of red embroidery thread, sew a running stitching following the outlines of the bird pattern (see Running Stitch on page 34). Repeat by stitching about ¼" (6mm) inside the first row of stitching. Continue stitching around the inside of each previous row of stitching until you reach the middle of the bird.

5 Finish design

Stitch in the bird's feet following the transferred pattern lines using the running stitch. Tie a knot on the inside of the vest to secure the embroidery floss.

Jazzed-Up Clothing

When you *restyle* a garment, you are not looking to be obvious with your transformation—you're looking for a complete transformation. In this chapter, you learn all about taking the plain and adding personality.

Many items can be made into completely different outfits by adding fabric and embellishments. As a bonus, you can save yourself from some tough sewing. In *Striped Floral T-Dress* (page 60), you'll learn how to take a plain T-shirt and transform it into a fun summer dress! By using scrap fabrics and making some strategic cuts, you can turn some clearance-rack winter pajamas into a cute summer sleeping ensemble with *Sleepover Makeover* (page 75).

When creating something unique, the wearer's needs should be paramount in your decision process. Be sure to consider the activities your little ones will be doing when restyling clothes for their wardrobe. Make it comfortable. Make it unique. Make it theirs!

Striped Floral T-Dress

Here is a sew-simple T-shirt dress you can whip up in a couple of hours. Choose your favorite fabrics and find a T-shirt to complement them, or use a T-shirt from the closet and take it to the fabric store to find fabric that fits the mood.

materials

T-shirt

Cutting mat

Ruler

Fabric marker

Rotary cutter

Sewing machine

Straight pins

Iron

½ yard (½m) print cotton or cotton blend fabric for skirt

½ yard (½m) of complementary print cotton or cotton-blend fabric for bias tape and pocket

¼" (6mm) wide fusible web tape

Needle

Thread

Assorted buttons

Ribbon

4⅜" snaps

Materials for the following Techniques:
- Getting Started with Fit (page 12)
- Garment Care and Handling (page 12)
- Bias Tape (page 17)
- Finishing a Raw Edge (page 20)
- Ruffles (page 21)
- Appliqué (page 30)

Deconstruction

1 Measure T-shirt

Choose a T-shirt the fits the intended wearer, concentrating on the fit around the neck and shoulder area (see Getting Started with Fit on page 12). Prepare the garment for use (see Garment Care and Handling on page 12).

Lay the T-shirt on the cutting mat. Using the fabric marker, mark each side of the shirt 3" (8cm) down from the armhole seam. Using the ruler, draw a line to connect the two dots.

2 Cut T-shirt

Using the rotary cutter, trim away the bottom portion of the T-shirt.

3 Mark armholes

Measure 2" (5cm) in from the top of the sleeve along the shoulder seam and place a mark. Make another mark just below the bottom of the armhole at the side seam. Draw a curved line connecting the two dots.

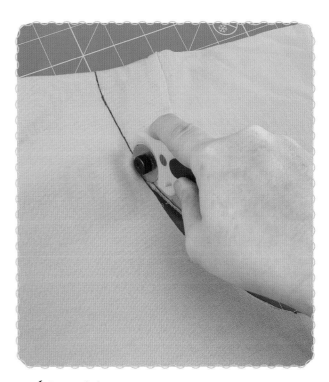

4 Cut armholes

Using the rotary cutter, trim along the curved line. Repeat steps 3 and 4 for the other sleeve.

5 Open side seams
Cut the T-shirt open along each of the side seams.

6 Staystitch cut edges
Staystitch along all freshly cut edges, being careful not to stretch the edges of the T-shirt. (Basting by hand is OK, too.)

Reconstruction

7 Bind edges
With the complementary fabric, make at least 2½ yards (2¼m) of bias tape (see Bias Tape on page 17). Encase the edges of the armholes and sides of the T-shirt with the bias tape. Use the sewing machine to stitch the bias tape onto the armholes.

8 Add bias tape to neckline
Pin a strip of the bias tape below the neckline seam and top-stitch along both edges, turning under the raw ends.

9 Begin skirt

To determine the length of the skirt: With the child wearing the trimmed T-shirt, measure from the bottom edge of the T-shirt to the desired hemmed length of the skirt. Add 4½" (11cm) to this number to allow for the seams and hem. This number is the length of the skirt panels.

To determine the width of the skirt panels: measure the bottom edge of the trimmed T-shirt, being careful not to stretch it too much.

Use the measurements to cut two skirt panels the lengths and widths calculated above. (Note: I cut two panels to allow fullness in the skirt.)

Cut four 5" (13cm) pieces of the bias tape. Starting at what will be the top edge of the skirt, encase the side seams along each of the skirt pieces.

10 Gather and attach skirt

Sew two rows of gathering stitches along the top edge of the skirt pieces at ⅜" (9mm) and ¼" (6mm) apart (see Ruffles on page 21). Pin the fabric skirt sections to the bottom edge of the T-shirt, right sides together. Stitch using a ½" (1cm) seam. Finish the seams (see Finishing a Raw Edge on page 20). Press the skirt down from the T-shirt top.

11 Prepare pocket

Cut a 5" × 7½" (13cm × 19cm) pocket (the pocket size was determined by the fabric image that was chosen; you may have a different size depending on the fabric design). Fold each of the sides and the bottom and top edge of the pocket under ½" (1cm) and press well.

12 Secure pocket

Turn the top edge under 1" (3cm) and topstitch the flap.

Set the pocket on the front of the skirt and topstitch close to the bottom and side edges. Leave the top unstitched.

13 Add bow
With the ribbon, tie a two-loop bow. Using the needle and thread, stitch the bow to the front top of the pocket.

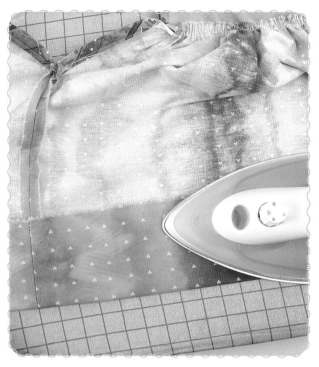

15 Prepare hem
With the fabric right side down, turn the hem under 3" (8cm) and press around the circumference of the skirt.

14 Sew skirt seams
Starting 4" (10cm) down from the top of the skirt, sew the side seams (you will be sewing the bottom 1" (3cm) of the bias tape placket you added in step 9).

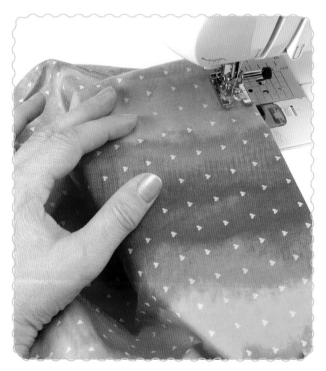

16 Stitch hem
Using the sewing machine, stitch ½" (1cm) from the pressed fold.

17 **Iron hem down**
Press the skirt hem down from the stitched tuck.

18 **Stitch hem details**
Sew three rows of stitching around the circumference of the hemline ½" (1cm), ¾" (2cm) and 1" (3cm) from the bottom of the skirt hem. (This will allow the hem to fray, but not too much.)

19 **Add appliqués and buttons**
Add the desired appliqués (see Appliqué on page 30). Sew a satin stitch along the edges of the appliqués.

Sew buttons on top of the neckline binding, creating interest and faux jewelry; on top of the pressed fold along the hemline; and on the front appliqué.

20 **Add snaps**
Sew snaps to the inside edge of the side openings of the shirt and skirt. Space the snaps along the opening of the side plackets with one at the top edge and the second near the bottom.

Rickrack Butterfly Skirt

If you have ever been to a thrift store, you've probably walked past curtain panels or fabric pieces hanging from racks. If you take the time to look through them you just might find the perfect item. I loved the rickrack on this piece and purchased it simply for that reason. It was not until I got home that I realized that with just a little sewing, a piece of elastic and some buttons, I could create a one-of-a-kind skirt perfect for the birthday girl next door.

materials

Window curtain or cotton shower curtain

Cutting mat

Rotary cutter

Sewing machine

Ruler

Iron

1" (3cm) wide elastic

Safety pin

½ yard (½m) white cotton cording

2 spring-loaded toggle closures

Needle

Thread

Assorted butterfly buttons

Materials for the following Techniques
• Getting Started with Fit (page 12)
• Finishing a Raw Edge (page 20)

Deconstruction

1 Measure fabric

You will need the following measurements to create this skirt: waist, hip and skirt length (see Getting Started with Fit on page 12).

Measure up from the bottom hemline of the curtain using the skirt length measurement plus 1¾" (4cm). If you prefer, trim the curtain to remove the bottom hemline, and then measure up from the new edge.

Multiply the hip measurement by 2, and add 1" (3cm) for the seams. Cut the curtain panel using this width.

Reconstruction

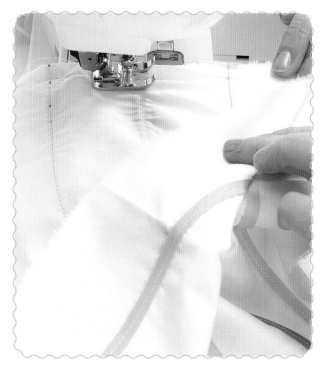

2 Sew side seam

Fold the curtain fabric in half, right sides together, and machine stitch the short ends together to create a basic skirt. Finish the raw edges of the seam (see Finishing a Raw Edge on page 20).

3 Prepare waist

Turn under the top edge of the skirt ¼" (6mm) and press. Turn under another 1¼" (3cm) and press well.

4 Stitch waist

Stitch close to the first folded edge leaving a 2" (5cm) opening near the seam line.

5 Add elastic

Cut a length of elastic using the waist measurement plus 1" (3cm). Insert the elastic through the casing at the top of the skirt using a large safety pin.

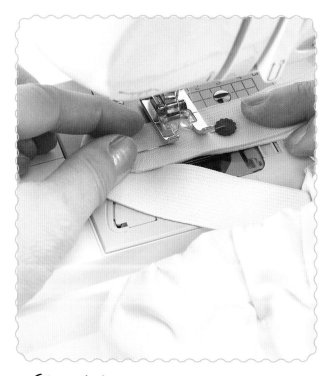

6 Secure elastic

Pull the elastic out of the hole (you'll redistribute the fabric later). Lap one end of the elastic over the other and stitch them together to secure.

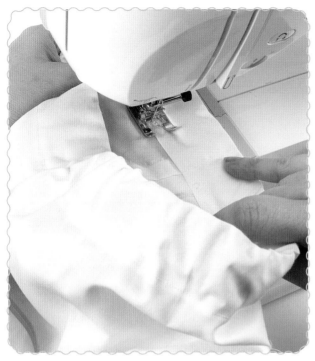

7 Finish waistband

Trim off any excess elastic. Redistribute the elastic inside the band. Stitch the 2" (5cm) opening closed, making sure not to catch the elastic in the seam.

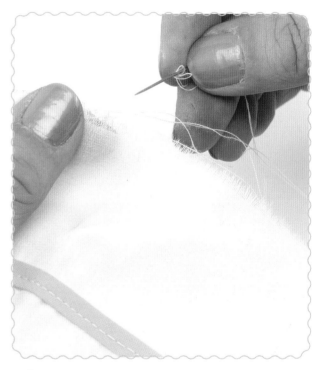

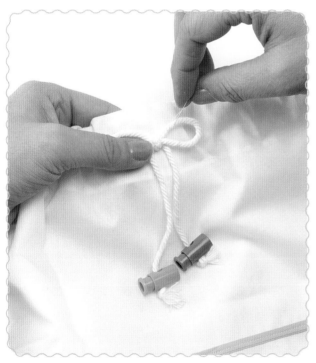

9 Finish skirt

Use the needle to loosen the crosswise threads along the hemline of the skirt. (Note: If your fabric choice does not have rickrack or some other stitched item, you will need to sew a row of decorative stitching 1" (3cm) above the hemline to prevent the raveling from continuing up the length of the skirt.)

Embellish with butterfly buttons, placing them randomly on the skirt front as desired.

8 Add bow embellishment

Using the cotton cording, tie a two-loop bow. Thread the spring toggles onto each end of the cording and tie overhand knots at each end of the cord. Using the needle and thread, stitch the bow to the center front of the skirt above the elastic casing.

Spring Ruffles

T-shirts are available at every turn, especially on clearance racks at the turn of each season. With the addition of a trio of ruffles created with complementary fabrics, that simple T-shirt becomes the perfect Easter dress for next year's Egg Roll at the White House or Easter Parade in your town.

materials

Long-sleeved empire waist white T-shirt

Cutting mat

Ruler

Fabric marker

Rotary cutter

Seam ripper

Straight pins

Sewing machine

Iron

Cotton or cotton-blend ½ yard (½m) each of two print fabrics, one pink and one blue

1 package white single fold bias tape

Three pink buttons

Plastic hair band

Needle

Thread

Glue

Materials for the following Techniques
- Getting Started with Fit (page 12)
- Bias Tape (page 17)
- Ties (page 18)
- Finishing a Raw Edge (page 20)
- Ruffles (page 21)
- Yo-Yos (page 26)

Deconstruction

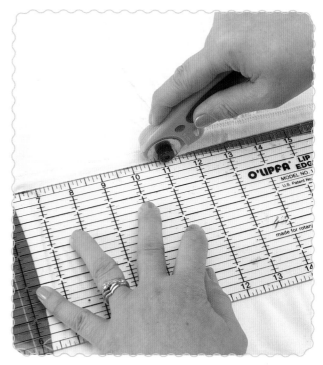

1 Prepare T-shirt
Choose a T-shirt that fits the intended wearer, concentrating on the fit around the neck and shoulder area. Lay the T-shirt on a flat surface. Using the ruler and the fabric marker, mark ½" (1cm) below the empire waist seam line.

2 Cut T-shirt
Using the rotary cutter, cut along the line, removing the bottom portion of the T-shirt.

3 Open side seams
Using the seam ripper, remove the stitching along the side seams 1" (3cm) up from each of the bottom edges of the T-shirt.

Reconstruction

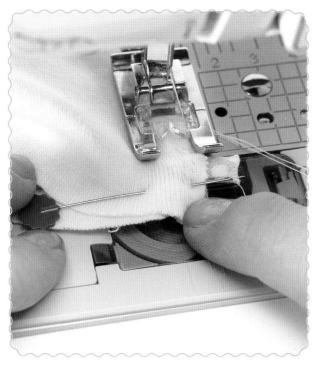

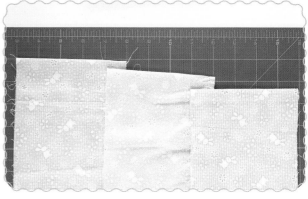

5 Prepare fabrics for skirt

To determine the length of the skirt: With the child wearing the trimmed T-shirt, measure down from the bottom edge of the T-shirt to the desired hemmed length of the skirt. Divide the number by 3 (or by the number of ruffles you want for the skirt). Add 1" (3cm) to this number.

4 Attach ties

Cut two strips of blue fabric 1¼" (3cm) wide by the width of the fabric, and use these to make two ties (see Ties on page 18).

Cut one of the finished ties in half. Pin the untied ends of the ties between the layers of the T-shirt at the side seam. Stitch the side seams of the T-shirt closed.

Set aside the other tie to be used as a front bow.

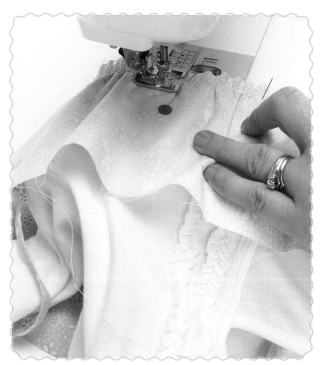

6 First ruffle

Use the measurement from step 5 (referred to as A) to cut the strips of fabric the measurement times the width of the fabric.

Cut one strip of pink fabric (A) × the width of fabric. With right-sides together, sew short ends together and press the seam open. Prepare a ruffle for this strip of fabric (see Ruffles on page 21).

Pin the ruffle to the bottom of the T-shirt, right sides together, and adjust the gathers. Stitch using a ½" (1cm) seam. Finish the raw edges (see Finishing a Raw Edge on page 20).

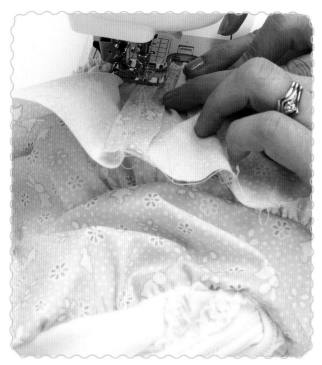

7 Complete ruffles

Repeat step 6 for the remaining two ruffles. For the second row of ruffles, use two strips of blue fabric sewn together. For the third row of ruffles, use two strips of pink fabric and one strip of blue fabric sewn together.

9 Embellish as desired

Embellish the skirt as desired. Using the tie created in step 4, I added a two-loop bow. Sewing buttons to the front of the dress always adds interest. Here, I also made a yo-yo with a pom-pom (see Yo-Yos on page 26).

8 Add binding

Encase the bottom of the third ruffle using purchased white bias tape. Stitch close to the folded edge of bias tape and overlap the bias tape's raw ends. Press well when you are finished stitching.

Hair band

10 **Create casing**
Cut a 3" × 30" (8cm × 76cm) wide strip from the pink fabric. Fold it in half, right sides together, and stitch using a ¼" (6mm) seam. Turn it right side out and press.

Topstitch ⅜" (9mm) away from each edge along the length of the strip.

Thread the hair band through the casing in the fabric strip, allowing the fabric to gather along the hair band.

12 **Create binding**
Cut a 3/4" (2cm) strip of blue fabric 1" (3cm) longer than the headband. Follow the Bias Tape steps 1–6 on page 17 to prepare the fabric.

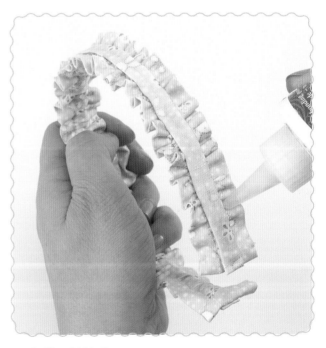

11 **Secure casing**
Turn under both ends of the casing and secure them with straight pins. Stitch through the ends of the hair band to attach the fabric.

13 **Add binding**
Turn under one end of the bias tape and glue it to the top of the hair band, over the pink ruffled band. Turn under the opposite end and glue. Let dry. Embellish the hair band as desired. I added a yo-yo with a pom-pom and a button.

Sleepover Makeover

Purchasing items out of season does not always pay off. Even the best guess at your child's size for next season can be thrown off with another growth spurt. If you're tired of the guessing game, try this: Buy the out-of-season clearance items in the size your child needs now and put your creative spin on them.

materials

Cotton stretch winter pajamas

Cutting mat

Ruler

Rotary cutter

Iron

Straight pins

½" (1cm) wide stretch gingham elastic

Sewing machine

½" (1cm) wide ribbon

2 ½" (1cm) buttons

Needle

Thread

Pencil

Scissors

Fusible web sheets

Cotton or cotton-blend fabric scraps for appliqué

Black gel pen fabric marker

Materials for the following Techniques
• Getting Started with Fit (page 12)
• Garment Care and Handling (page 12)
• Finishing a Raw Edge (page 20)
• Ruffles (page 21)
• Appliqué (page 30)

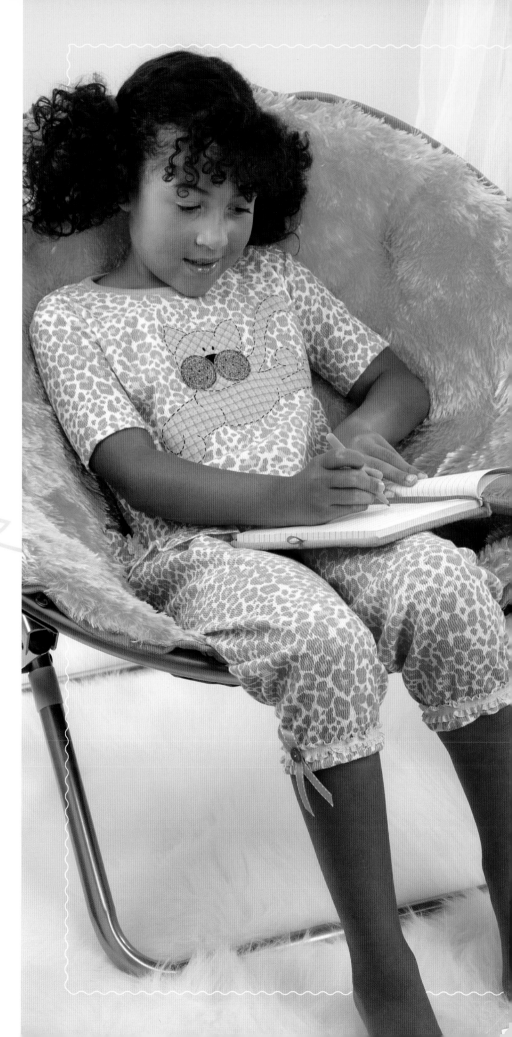

Deconstruction

1 Prepare top

Purchase a two-piece pajama set that fits the intended wearer comfortably (see Getting Started with Fit on page 12). Prepare the pajamas for use (see Garment Care and Handling on page 12).

Lay the pajama top on the top of the cutting mat, aligning the bottom hemline along the horizontal grid line of the mat. Measure up 5" (13cm) from the bottom hemline. Using the ruler and rotary cutter, cut along this line, removing the bottom portion of the pajama top.

Cut two 2" (5cm) strips from the portion of the pajamas top you just removed.

Align the side seams of the pajama top with a vertical grid line on the cutting mat. Lay the ruler even with the side seam and 5" (13cm) from the underarm seam. Cut along this line, removing the bottom portion of the pajama sleeve.

Repeat for the other sleeve. Discard the removed sleeve pieces.

2 Prepare bottoms

Lay the pajama bottoms on the cutting mat, aligning each of the bottom cuffs along the horizontal grid line of the mat. Measure up 5" (13cm) from the top of the cuff. Cut along this line, removing the bottom portion of each of the pajama legs.

Reconstruction

3 Press bottoms hem
Turn the bottom edge of each of the pajama legs under 1" (3cm). Using the iron, press the folded fabric.

5 Add embellishments
Cut two 5" (13cm) pieces of ribbon. Fold each piece into a bow and stitch one to the side of each leg. Sew a button to the center of each bow.

4 Add gingham trim
Using straight pins, secure a length of gingham elastic trim on the outside of the pajama leg. Starting at the inside side seam, align it with the turned-under hem. Using a stretch stitch on the sewing machine, stitch the elastic to the hem. Slightly pull the elastic as you sew to achieve a slight gather. Overlap the ends and stitch.

6 Add bow
Tie a 12" (30cm) section of ribbon into a two-loop bow. Stitch it to the center front of the pajama bottoms.

TIP

The smaller openings of sleeves and legs can be hard to stitch using the sewing machine. If you are able, use the open arm feature of the sewing machine to fit the sleeve over it.

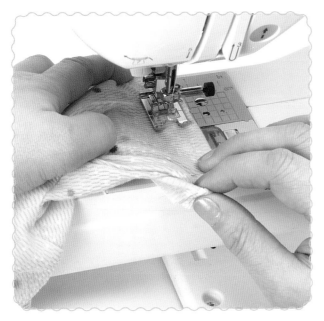

7 Hem sleeves

Turn under 1" (3cm) along the bottom edge of the sleeves. Stitch using a stretch stitch on the sewing machine. After stitching, press the hem with the iron.

8 Create ruffles

Using the 2" (5cm) pieces of fabric from step 1, create a ruffle (see Ruffles on page 21). Pin the ruffles to the bottom hemline of the pajama top, right sides together. Pull the gathering threads and adjust the ruffle as you pin. Stitch the ruffle to the shirt bottom using a ½" (1cm) seam. Finish the edges using a serger or an overcast stitch (see Finishing a Raw Edge on page 20).

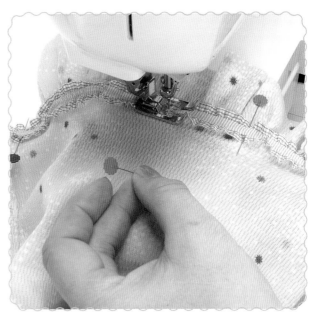

9 Add gingham trim

Cut a piece of gingham elastic trim about an inch longer than what is needed to circle the bottom of the shirt, just above the ruffle. Pin the gingham elastic trim to the top of the stitching on the right side of the pajama top. Stitch using a stretch stitch on the sewing machine. Overlap the ends and stitch.

10 Add appliqué

Embellish the front of the pajama top with the fabric appliqué (see Appliqué on page 30). Using the fabric gel pen, add highlights and pen-stitching lines to the top of the appliqué. Follow the manufacturer's instructions to set the ink.

Mod Floral Jacket and Leggings

Transform a basic white T-shirt into a fun jacket inspired by your fabric choice. Need to dress up a simple pair of black leggings? One of my favorite ways is to add some button art. Stitching on buttons is an easy embellishment; create crazy flowers or curve meandering vines up a pant leg or sleeve.

materials

Long-sleeved T-shirt

Iron

Scissors

Cutting mat

Ruler

Rotary cutter

Measuring tape

Sewing machine

1 yard (1m) cotton or cotton-blend fabric

Straight pins

⅛ yard (11cm) coordinating print fabric for pockets

Assorted buttons

Needle

Thread

Leggings

Fabric glue

½" (1cm) wide elastic

Materials for the following Techniques:
- Getting Started with Fit (page 12)
- Garment Care and Handling (page 12)
- Finishing a Raw Edge (page 20)
- Ruffles (page 21)
- Prairie Points (page 28)
- Adding Buttons (page 32)

Deconstruction

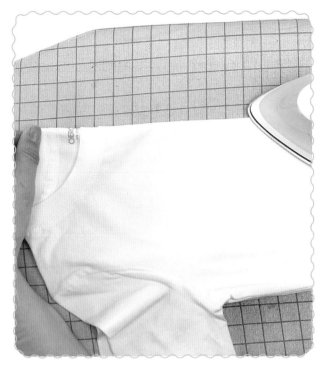

1 Fold T-shirt in half

Choose a T-shirt that fits the intended wearer, concentrating on a fit that will allow a light T-shirt to be layered underneath. Prepare the garment for use (see Garment Care and Handling on page 12).

Fold the T-shirt in half vertically and press a line down the center front of the shirt.

3 Trim sleeves

Lay the T-shirt right side up on top of the cutting mat and align the ruler along the outside edge to one of the sleeves. Adjust the ruler so it measures 3" (8cm) down from the bottom edge of the armhole. Using the rotary cutter, cut across the sleeve, removing the lower portion. Repeat this step for the other sleeve.

2 Cut T-shirt open

Cut the T-shirt front open along this pressed line.

Reconstruction

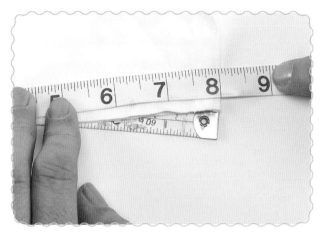

4 Measure sleeve opening

Measure the T-shirt sleeve opening. Double this number and add 1" (3cm) to the total. (In this case, I came up with 9" [23cm].)

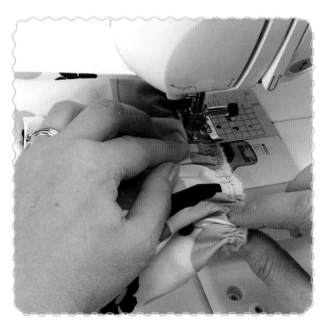

5 Create ruffle cuff

Using the measurement from step 4, cut two pieces of fabric 10" (25cm) in length × the measurement. Create two folded ruffles (see Ruffles on page 21).

Insert the T-shirt sleeve into the fabric sleeve, right sides together, matching the seams and raw edges. Pull the gathering threads to distribute the gathers evenly around the sleeve and pin. Stitch the sleeve and ruffle together using a ½" (1cm) seam.

Finish the raw edges (see Finishing a Raw Edge on page 20). Press the ruffle down from the T-shirt sleeve.

TIP

Be careful not to stretch the T-shirt sleeve during this process.

6 Add prairie points

Create five prairie point squares using 4" (10cm) squares of the main fabric (see Prairie Points, steps 1–2, on page 28).

Align the prairie points with edges of the opening you created in step 2, three on one side and two on the other. Space the points so, when folded under ½" (1cm), the points cross over each other and lay flat on the opposite side. Pin the points in place.

7 Add fabric strips

Cut a 2" (5cm) wide strip of fabric. Flip the fabric strip so the right sides of the strip and the T-shirt are together. Turn the top edge of the fabric strip ½" (1cm) to the right side and pin it to the neckline of the T-shirt. Starting at the top of the neckline of the T-shirt pin the strip right sides together along the front edge of the T-shirt, covering the prairie points.

Continue pinning until you reach the bottom edge of the T-shirt. Trim the strip ½" (1cm) longer than the T-shirt and then fold it back over the end of the pinned strip. Repeat this step along the opposite side of the T-shirt opening.

8 Stitch prairie points
Stitch through the front fabric layers using a ½" (1cm) seam.

9 Trim prairie points
Using the ruler and rotary cutter, trim off the prairie points from the inside.

10 Press facings
Fold the facings to the inside of the T-shirt, allowing the prairie points to extend out from the T-shirt edges and press. Turn under ¼" (6mm) along each of the raw edges of the facings and press. Pin to hold in place.

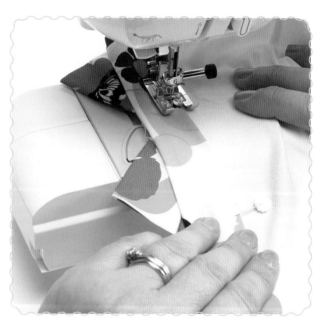

11 Stitch facings
Topstitch through all layers of the facing and T-shirt fronts.

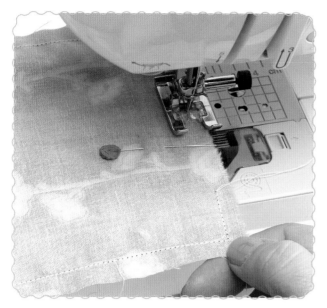

12 Prepare pocket

Cut a 5" (13cm) square from the main fabric and a 5" (13cm) square from the coordinating fabric. Lay the fabric squares right sides together and pin. Stitch them together using a ¼" (6mm) seam and leaving a 2" (5cm) opening along one side.

13 Trim corners

Using the scissors, trim the corners of the pocket squares.

14 Iron pocket flap

Turn the pocket right side out and press. Turn the square on point and fold down the top point to form a flap. The 2" (5cm) opening should be opposite this pocket flap. Iron the fold.

Repeat steps 12–14 for the second pocket.

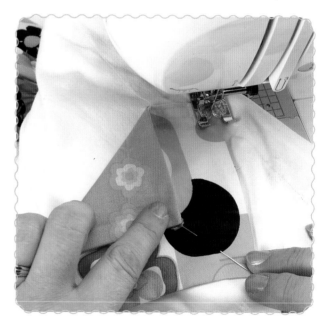

15 Attach pockets

Pin the pockets to the front of the T-shirt using the project photo as a guide for placement. Stitch the pockets to the T-shirt.

TIP

*As you stitch the pockets to the T-shirt,
the 2" (5cm) opening will be stitched closed.*

16 Add buttons

Sew a button to the center front of the pocket flaps; three buttons to each of the front edges starting at the neckline and working down; and a black button to the center top of each sleeve (see Adding Buttons on page 32).

17 Leggings

Lay the leggings on a flat surface and place the buttons onto the pant legs, either following the project photo as a guide for placement or creating your own design. Secure the buttons (see Adding Buttons on page 32).

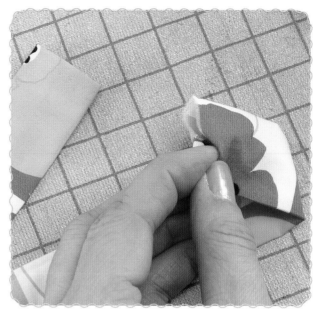

18 Prepare headband

Cut one 3¼" × 17" (8cm × 43cm) rectangle in the main fabric. With the right sides together, fold the 17" (43cm) length of fabric in half and stitch using a ¼" (6mm) seam. Press the seam open and turn right side out. Press the fabric well.

Turn the ends in ¼" (6mm) and press.

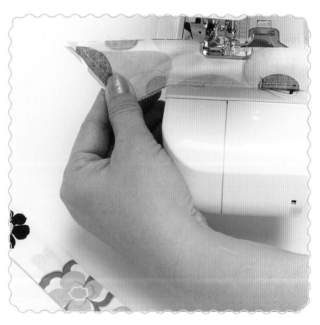

19 Prepare headband ties

Cut four 1¼" × 7" (3cm × 18cm) rectangles in the main fabric. With one set of 7" (18cm) rectangles laying right sides together, trim one end at a diagonal. Repeat for the other piece.

Stitch each of the sets of trimmed rectangles together, using a ¼" (6mm) seam and leaving the end open.

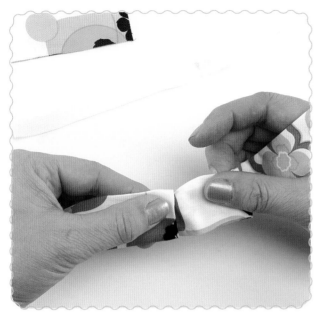

20 Assemble headband

Turn the ties right side out and press. Cut a 5" (13cm) piece of ½" (1cm) elastic. With the seam line of the 17" (43cm) section of the head band facing up, insert the straight end of one tie end into the open band end.

22 Complete headband

Stitch through all the layers to secure the end.
Sew buttons to the center top of the headband for added interest.

21 Secure pieces

Center the elastic over the tie end and insert it into the band. Stitch through all the layers to secure the end. Have the intended wearer try on the headband and mark the elastic where it comfortably fits into the opposite open end of the band.
Using the straight pins, secure the headband pieces.

Embellished Accessories

It's not just Hand-Me-Ups clothing that can add a punch to your child's wardrobe. Hand-Me-Ups accessories will, too! From head to toe, you'll learn how to add to the extras that add fun to getting dressed.

Start at the top with the *Beaded and Stamped Visor* (page 106) and the *Painted Baseball Cap* (page 108). Help your kids carry through the day with the *Autograph Backpack* (page 110). Put some bounce in their step with four cute shoe projects and so much more. This chapter is full of fun!

Designed for their impact, these projects offer lots of chances for the little ones to help, and they make great gifts for giving. Choose one and start today!

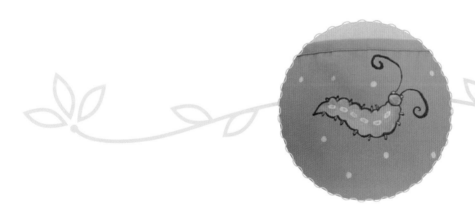

Stamped Frame Jewelry

What outfit is really complete without the addition of a piece of jewelry? Make it personal, make it yourself. The stamp and beads are your choice; follow the step-by-step instructions to create a fun and inexpensive jewelry collectible.

materials

Mini frame stamps (find them in the scrapbooking supplies)

Pigment ink stamp option pad

Stampable shrink plastic

Ruler

1¼" (3cm) square punch

Flower hole punch

Heat gun

Stylus

1 package ¼" (6mm) jump rings

Needle-nose pliers

1 package ½" (1cm) plastic flower beads

1mm wide stretch elastic cording

Scissors

1 package assorted glass E beads

Beacon 527 multi-use glue

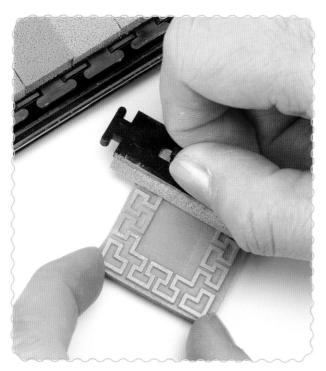

1 Ink stamp
Choose a color from the stamp option pad and ink the stamp.

2 Stamp shrink plastic
Stamp the images directly onto the shrink plastic, leaving a ¼" (6mm) space between each of the images. Repeat steps 1 and 2 to use all of the colors available in the stamp option pad.

3 Punch out image
Using the square punch, center the image in the punch and punch out the image.

4 Punch corner holes

Using the flower hole punch, punch a hole at one corner of each square, approximately ¼" (6mm) in from the corner. Repeat steps 1–4 for 16 shrink plastic pieces.

5 Shrink design

Following the directions provided with the stampable shrink plastic, shrink the plastic on a heat-resistant surface. Use a stylus in the punched hole so the shrink wrap doesn't fly away while heating. Don't worry if the plastic curls on one side; just keep applying a steady amount of heat and it will straighten itself out.

6 Add charms and beads to jump rings

Using the needle-nose pliers, open each of the jump rings in a scissor fashion. Thread a shrink charm onto the ring and close the ring. Repeat until all charms have rings attached to them. Follow this step to add the flower beads to the 18 jump rings. Note: The number of jump rings, flower beads and glass E beads will vary depending on the size and design of your necklace.

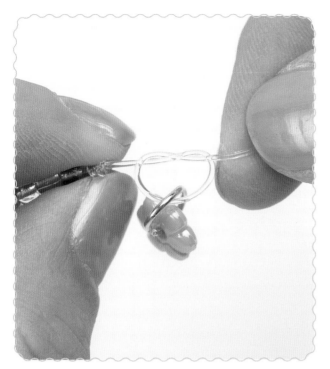

7 Assemble necklace

Using the scissors, cut a 28" (71cm) length of elastic cording and tie a knot at one end. Thread four E beads onto the cording. Thread a jump ring bead onto the cording. Slide the jump ring up to the beads and tie a knot over the top of the jump ring to hold the ring in place.

Thread four E beads onto the cording. Thread a jump ring charm onto the cording. Slide the jump ring up to the beads and tie a knot over the top of the jump ring to hold the ring in place.

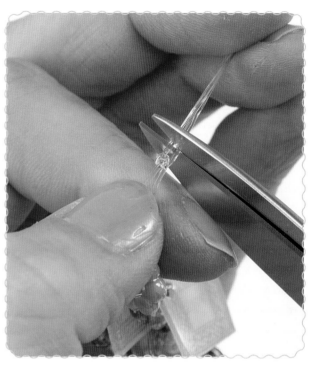

9 Trim cording

Using the scissors, trim the excess cording.

8 Secure ends

Repeat step 7 until the necklace reaches 22" (56cm) in length. Tie the cord ends together in a knot a couple of times, pulling the cords taught.

Add a drop of glue to the knot and let it dry.

Timely Tags

Check your baggage with style. Colorful and personal, these tags will leave no question as to who your luggage belongs to. Show off your child's style, colors and favorite things.

materials

Stiffened felt in colors of your choice

Scissors

Sewing machine

Fabric glue

Brads

Ribbon or cording

**Embellishments such as
small buttons and embroidery thread**

Materials for the following Technique
• Creating and Transferring a Pattern (page 13)

1 Create pattern

Use your computer to access a font program that fits your needs. Enlarge the desired letter and print it on your printer. Transfer the letter to the stiffened felt (see Creating and Transferring a Pattern on page 13).

Using the scissors, cut out the letter.

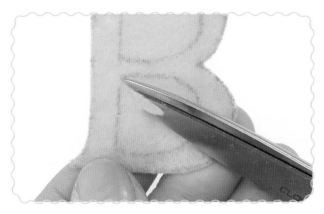

2 Cut trapped spaces

To cut the inside spaces, poke a hole in the center. Cut out from there.

 TIP

Using a Sizzix Die Cut machine makes fast work of monogrammed tags. Just use the machine in place of steps 1 and 2, and for any embellishments in step 4.

3 Add background

Using the basic tag patterns provided (see the CD for the patterns), cut out a piece of stiffened felt for the front of the tag. Layer the monogram on the front piece. Using the sewing machine, stitch through both layers to secure them.

4 Add embellishment

Cut out additional design elements such as flowers, scrolls and other decorative touches using the patterns provided (see the CD). Either glue the designs to the front of the tag or attach them with a brad.

5 Add backing

Using the basic tag patterns provided, cut out a piece of stiffened felt for the back of the tag. Spread glue on the back piece. Set the front tag on top of the back tag and press together. Lift the top edge of the tag and insert a section of ribbon or cording that has been folded in half. Press the flaps together. Set the tag under a heavy, flat object to dry.

If desired, add additional interest by sewing buttons to the corners using a needle and embroidery floss.

Wrapped Yarn Bangles and Headband

What could be simpler, yet so trendy as wrapped yarn accessories? Choose a yarn that fits the mood and wrap away. This is a great kid project, simple enough for even the youngest designer-in-the-making to create and wear.

materials

Wooden or plastic bangle

Headband

Yarn

Scissors

Fabric glue

Bangles

1 Prepare yarn
Using the scissors, cut an 8 yard (7m) length of yarn and wrap it into a small ball. Tie the end around the bangle using a double knot.

2 Wrap bangle
Wrap the yarn around the bangle, threading the ball of yarn through the inside of the bangle. Wrap the yarn tightly with each wrap close to the preceding one.

3 Secure yarn
Continue wrapping the yarn around until the entire bangle is covered. If desired, continue wrapping the bangle to cover any open areas or to achieve a fuller look.

Thread the yarn end under the last couple of wraps. Add a drop of glue and let it dry. Trim away the excess yarn.

Headband

4 Prepare yarn
Cut a 6 yard (5½m) length of yarn and roll it into a small ball for easy use when wrapping your headband.

Lay the yarn end over the bottom end of the headband to cover the end.

5 Wrap headband
Wrap the yarn around the headband covering the yarn end. Continue wrapping the yarn around the headband until the entire headband is covered (you will double wrap over the end of the headband). Wrap the yarn tightly with each wrap close to the preceding one.

6 Finish ends
When you reach the opposite side, cover the end piece with the yarn and begin wrapping up the opposite direction until the headband is completely covered. If desired, continue wrapping the headband to cover any open areas or to achieve a fuller look.

Thread the yarn end under the last couple of wraps. Add a drop of glue and let it dry. Trim away the excess yarn.

Flip-Flop Fantasy

Summer would not be summer without a pair of flip-flops. Create a pair that will stand out in the crowd with the addition of some brightly colored ribbon and a bow. Inexpensive footwear does not have to be plain.

materials

Flip-flops

Fabric glue

½" (1cm) wide ribbon

Scissors

Awl or pointed tool such as a large needle

Brads

Two buttons

Needle

Thread

Paint pen

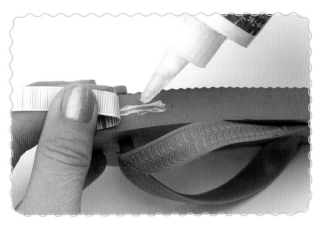

1 Add ribbon

Beginning at the center back edge of the flip-flop, apply a small amount of glue to the back of the ribbon, working around the flip-flop, pressing the ribbon against the side of the flip-flop, holding it in place until the glue is tacky.

2 Mark holes for brads

Beginning where the ribbon overlaps, use the scissors to trim the ribbon so it overlaps about ½" (1cm). Use the awl or large needle to poke holes through the ribbon and into the side of the flip-flop where you want to insert the brads.

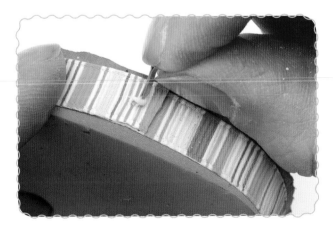

3 Attach brads

Dip the end of the brad into glue and insert it into a hole.
Repeat this step until you've placed the desired amount of brads. Let the glue dry.

4 Add ribbon to strap

Glue the ribbon to the top of the flip-flop straps. Using the awl or large needle, tuck and glue the raw edges into the flip-flop base.

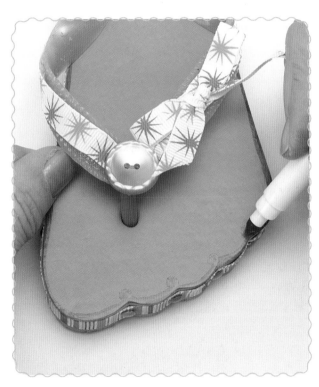

5 Embellish flip-flops

Embellish the flip-flop as desired. Here, I glued a bow to the top of the flip-flop strap and used a needle and thread to sew a button to the center top of each flip-flop. (You can sew through the rubber; just push!) I also used the paint marker to add dots and lines to the edge of the flip-flop.

Repeat steps 1–5 for the other flip-flop.

All-Buttoned-Up Canvas Slip-Ons

Once again, buttons are the key to dressing up even the most basic wearable items. Pull out those shoes from the back of the closet, dust them off and add a couple of buttons. Voilà! The old shoes become new and fun.

materials

Canvas slip-on shoes

Coral shell buttons in 1" (3cm), ¾" (2cm) and ½" (1cm)

Fabric glue

Needle

Navy blue thread

Materials for the following Technique
• Adding Buttons (page 32)

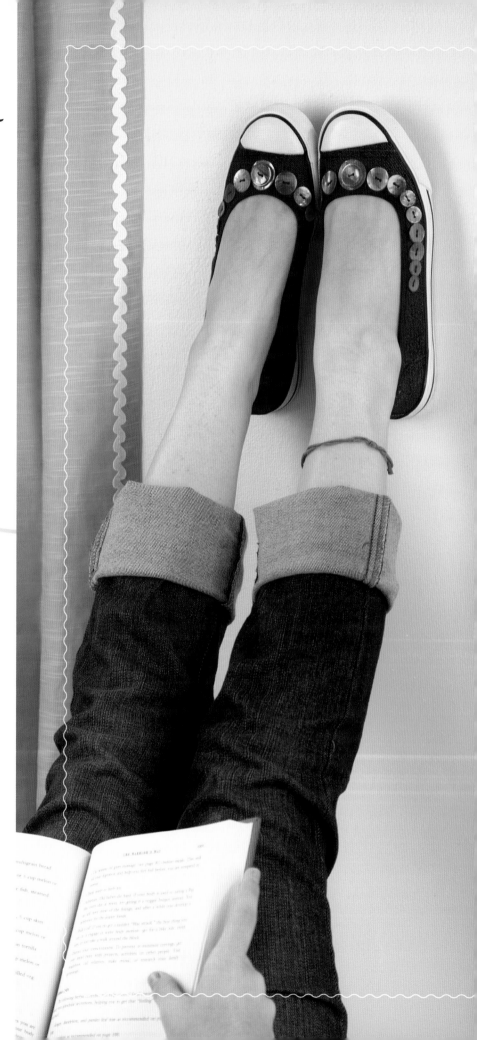

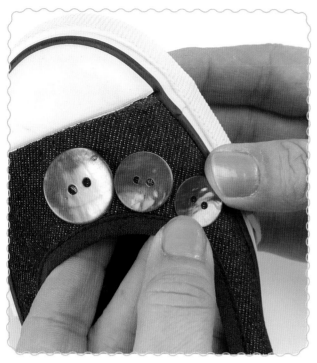

1 Lay out button design

Place the shoes on a flat surface and position the buttons on the top of the shoes in the desired pattern. You can refer to the project photo for button placement, but consider changing up the design to customize your choice of shoes.

3 Stitch buttons

Using the needle and navy blue thread, stitch the buttons to the shoes. Each button should be stitched onto the shoe individually, tying off the thread before staring with a new button.

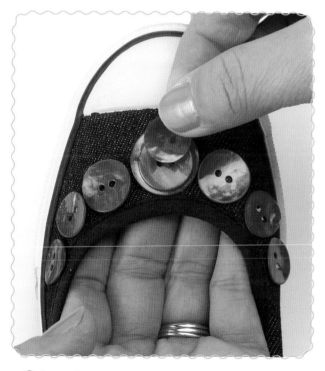

2 Secure buttons

When you are happy with the layout, secure the buttons with glue, avoiding the holes (see Adding Buttons on page 32). Repeat until all buttons have been glued in place.

The center front buttons have been stacked to create an interesting look. Start with a 1" (3cm) button then layer a ¾" (2cm) and end with a ½" (1cm) button. Align the holes of all three buttons and secure them with glue.

Painted Lace-Up Boots

A pair of thrift store lace-up boots cross the line into a sought-after fashion accessory with the addition of craft paint and some brushstrokes. The transformation is quick, and you will achieve instant gratification as soon as you hear the first exclamation of "Where did you find those boots?"

materials

Boots

Damp cloth

Fabric Paint in blue, white, pink, green and yellow

1" (3cm) sponge brush

Paintbrushes in No. 0 liner, No. 5 round and No. 4 shader

Sponge

Matte varnish spray

2 yards (2m) ¼" (6mm) wide checked ribbon

Scissors

Supplies for the following Technique
• Painting on Fabric (page 15)

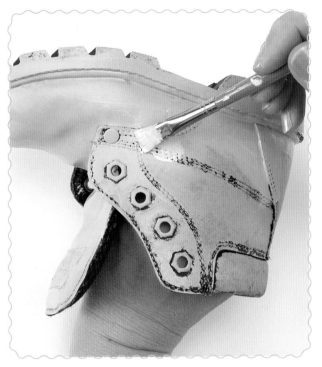

1 Prepare boots

Remove the boots' shoelaces and set them aside. Clean the boots well using a damp cloth and let them dry overnight. Prepare your work surface (see step 1 of Painting on Fabric on page 15).

Using the sponge brush, paint the boots with the blue paint. Repeat for opaque coverage. Use a stiff-bristled paintbrush to paint into the leather surface and let it dry well between coats of paint.

2 Add green grass and highlights

Dip the sponge into the green paint. Lightly tap the sponge along the bottom edge of the boots and along the edges of the soles. Let the paint dry thoroughly.

Using the sponge, lightly sponge the white paint along the top of the green paint. Let the paint dry thoroughly.

3 Add grass

Using the liner brush and green paint, stroke in flower stems and individual grass blades.

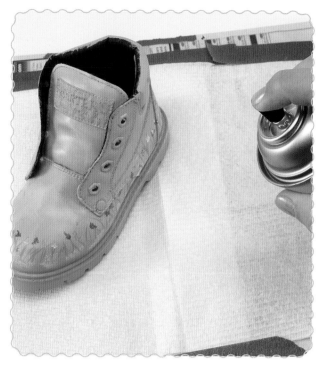

4 Add flowers

Dip the round brush into the pink paint, and then dip the tip of the brush into the white paint. Dab the paint to the tops of some of the stems, forming flowers. Continue working around the circumference of the boots adding flowers to the stems. Let the paint dry thoroughly.

Repeat this step using the yellow paint.

5 Coat boots with varnish

In a well-ventilated area, spray the boots with two coats of matte varnish. Let the varnish dry between coats.

6 Add laces

Cut two lengths of ribbon the same length as the laces removed from the boots in step 1. Lace up the boots. Tie each of the ribbon ends in an overhand knot. Trim the ends at a 45-degree angle. Tie the ribbon laces as you would any other shoe lace.

Crocodile Clogs

More and more you can find inexpensive children's footwear for children just waiting to be embellished. These inexpensive clogs make a great project for the kids to either complete on their own with a little supervision in a class session, or perhaps as a family or team project.

materials

Clogs

Measuring tape

¼" (6mm) hole punch

Large plastic yarn needle

1 yard (1m) of ⅛" (3mm) wide ribbon

Scissors

Paint markers in assorted colors

1 Mark holes

Starting at the center front and using the measuring tape, mark the shoes at ½" (1cm) increments with the paint markers.

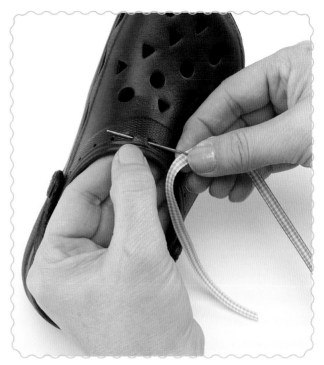

3 Start threading ribbon

Thread the ribbon through the yarn needle. Beginning right of center on the front, insert the needle through the hole, coming out of the center hole.

2 Punch holes

Mark two holes in the center back of the strap a ½" (1cm) apart.

Using the hole punch, punch where you marked with the paint pen in steps 1 and 2.

4 Thread ribbon through holes

Pull the ribbon through, leaving an 8" (20cm) tail. Stitch down the side of the shoe. When you reach the final hole, return back to the center, bringing the ribbon up through the opposite holes.

5 Thread through opposite side

When you reach the center, work the ribbon across and down the opposite side. Repeat step 4 to return to the center.

7 Add back bow

Thread the needle with ribbon and thread the ribbon through the holes in the back strap. Trim the ribbon ends to equal lengths and tie it into a bow.

6 Finish tie

When you reach the center, use the scissors to trim the ribbon equal to the ribbon tail.

Tie a knot and a bow.

8 Paint design

Using the paint pens, design the shoe. Here, I mimicked the scallop design of the clog. Continue to embellish as desired.

Repeat steps 1–8 for the other shoe.

Beaded and Stamped Visor

Dress up an inexpensive foam visor with beads and stamping techniques. Choose a favorite stamped image and some plastic beads and have fun. The range of possibilities is endless. Perhaps a team or troop logo or a family reunion theme is the ticket. This makes a great class or fun children's project.

materials

Craft foam visor

Measuring tape

Pencil

¹⁄₁₆" (2mm) hole punch

Large-eyed needle

White pearl cotton

Scissors

Plastic floral beads

Glue

Whimsical floral stamp

Hot pink stamp pad

Cotton swab

Materials for the following Technique
• Backstitch with Beading (page 35)

1 Mark holes

Using the measuring tape and the pencil, start at the middle front of the visor and mark ½" (1cm) spaces about ¼" (6mm) up from the edge of the visor.

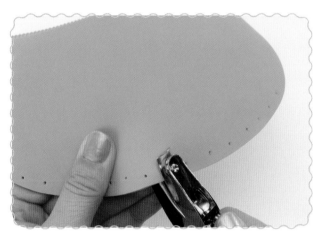

2 Punch holes

Use the hole punch to create holes.

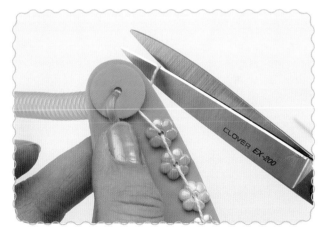

3 Add beads

Thread the needle with an 18" (46cm) length of pearl cotton. Add the beads (see Backstitch with Beading on page 35), using the punched holes as your guide.

When you reach the end, thread the pearl cotton to the bottom of the visor and secure it with a knot. Add a drop of glue to the knot. Using the scissors, trim the excess pearl cotton.

4 Add stamps

Carefully ink the stamp and stamp the floral design, centering it on the visor front. Stamp additional images as desired.

5 Add dots

Create dots using the cotton swab and the ink pad.

Painted Baseball Cap

Pretty in pink, while still looking sporty, is the ticket with this design. A simple white baseball cap is embellished with gingham bias tape and a painted rose. Simple coloring book painting techniques are easy to follow. Why not paint two for a mom-and-me fashion statement?

materials

White cotton baseball cap

¼ yard (23cm) cotton or cotton blend fabric for bias tape

Fabric paint in pink, white, black and green

Paintbrushes in No. 0 liner and No. 5 round

Bowl of water

Black fabric marker

Fabric glue

Cotton swab

Materials for the following Techniques
- Creating and Transferring a Pattern (page 13)
- Painting on Fabric (page 15)
- Bias Tape (page 17)

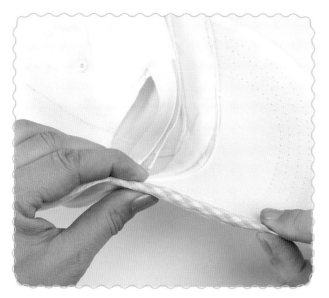

1 Add bias tape

Make 18" (46cm) of wide fabric bias tape (see Bias Tape on page 17). Trim the bias tape at an angle to match it to the edge where the bill of the cap meets the crown. Carefully spread fabric glue along the inside of the bias tape, working with 3" (8cm) sections at a time.

Press the bias tape into place along the edge of the bill. Add additional glue to the end. Continue until the bill is entirely encased in bias tape. Trim the opposite edge similar to the starting point.

2 Transfer pattern

Transfer the pattern (see the CD) to the baseball cap using the project photo as a guide for placement (see Creating and Transferring a Pattern on page 13).

Using the round brush, paint the stems and leaves using green paint. Streak some white paint through the wet paint. Let the paint dry thoroughly. Use the bowl of water to rinse the brushes as needed.

TIP

Using straight pins helps to hold the pattern in place while transferring.

3 Add petals

Paint the petals using pink with white stroked through the wet paint. (Leave a small space between petals to help with petal separation.) Let the paint dry.

4 Add outline

Using the fabric marker for straight lines and the liner brush with black paint for the curvy lines, outline the design. Let the paint dry thoroughly before wearing.

Autograph Backpack

I look out my front window each weekday morning to see my friend and neighbor, Sierra, heading off to preschool. I would like her to know that her friends and family are thinking about her all day long so I decided to send our thoughts and wishes with her to school each day on this simple button-adorned backpack.

materials

Canvas mini backpack

Disappearing fabric marking pen

Assorted buttons in sizes ¼"– 1" (6mm–3cm)

Black embroidery floss

Fabric glue

Embroidery needle

Stiffened felt in white and lime green

10" (25cm) piece of black-and-white cording

Black gel roller fabric marking pen

Materials for the following Techniques
- Creating and Transferring a Pattern (page 13)
- Adding Buttons (page 32)
- Running Stitch (page 34)

1 Plan design

Use the disappearing fabric marking pen to draw in stems, leaves and curly lines onto the canvas backpack.

Use the project photo as a guide for button placement. Lay buttons onto the front and side panels of the backpack. When you are happy with the arrangement, secure the buttons (see Adding Buttons on page 32).

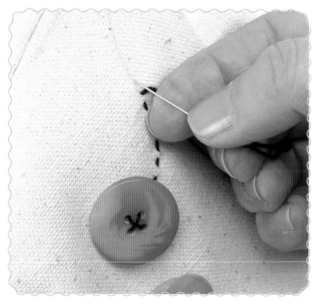

2 Add embroidery

Thread the embroidery needle with an 18" (46cm) length of the embroidery floss. Sew the buttons onto the bag.

Sew along each of the drawn lines using a running stitch (see Running Stitch on page 34).

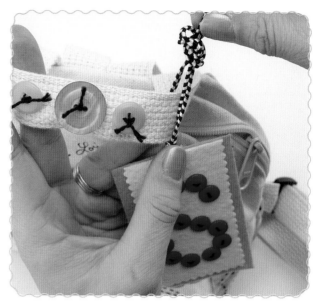

3 Create and add tag

Create a tag with the intended child's initial using the felt and the black-and-white cording (see *Timely Tags* on page 92). Tie the tag around the top strap of the backpack.

4 Add fun sayings

Using the black gel marking pen, have friends and family write inspirational and personal messages directly onto the top, sides and back panels of the backpack. Follow the manufacturer's instructions to set the ink.

Ideas for Messages

100% Girl, Baby Girl, Daddy's Little Princess,
Girls just wanna have fun!, Genuine Girl, Classy & Sassy

Techno-Fun Tote

Whether heading to Grandma's house, a sleepover or a play date, kids just wanna have fun. The choice of fun fabrics is limitless; check out the retro rockets and space-age pets on this combination of prints.

materials

Tote

½ yard (½m) fabric (print A)

½ yard (½m) fabric (print B)

¼ yard (¼m) fabric (print C)

Scissors

Iron

Sewing machine

Cutting mat

Rotary cutter

Ruler

Straight pins

Buttons

Needle

Thread

Fusible web

Polyester batting scrap

Grommet

Grommet setter

12" (30cm) nylon cording

Materials for the following Techniques
- Prairie Points (page 28)
- Adding Buttons (page 32)

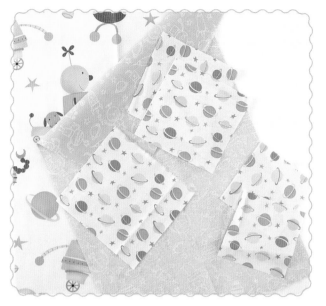

1 Prepare fabric pieces

Cut the following:

Print A: 12" × 20" (30cm × 51cm) for a pocket.

Print B: 12" × 20" (30cm × 51cm) for a pocket; 6" (15cm) square for the fabric lining.

Print C: 6" (15cm) square for the tab; one 6" (15cm), two 5" (13cm) squares and two 4" (10cm) squares for prairie points.

2 Assemble fabric pieces

Using the smaller squares of fabric, make prairie points (see Prairie Points on page 28).

Using the diagram as a guide (see the CD) fold the prairie points squares into triangles and overlap them to form a border row fitting the top edge of the pocket. Allow for ½" (1cm) side seams. Pin the border to the top edge of the pocket lining.

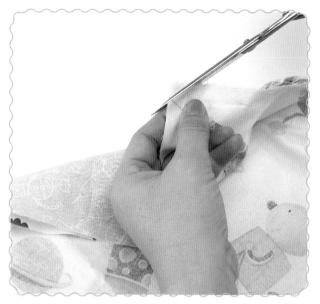

3 Stitch pocket

Sew the two pocket pieces together, right sides together, using a ½" (1cm) seam and leaving a 3" (8cm) opening along one edge. Using the scissors, trim the corners.

4 Press pocket

Turn the pocket right side out and press.

5 Prepare fabric triangle

Set the two 6" (15cm) tab squares on top of each other, right sides together, on the cutting mat. Cut diagonally across the squares. Pin one set of triangles together (the other set will not be used).

6 Stitch triangle

Stitch around the circumference of the triangles using a ¼" (6mm) seam and leaving a 2" (5cm) opening along the bottom of the triangle. Using the scissors, trim the corners. Turn right side out and press.

7 Add pocket and triangle to bag

Turn over the top edge of the pocket 4½" (11cm), forming a flap, and press well.

Center the triangle along the bottom edge of the pocket and pin it to the pocket. Pin the pocket to the front of the bag.

· ⟨ · ⟨ · ⟨ · ⟨ · ⟨ ❀ TIP ❀ ⟩ · ⟩ · ⟩ · ⟩ · ⟩ ·

Using the open-arm feature on your sewing machine (if available) is a great way to keep the back of the bag from being caught in the sewing process.

8 Stitch pocket to bag

Topstitch close to the sides and bottom of the pocket. Stitch the pocket again, this time stitching ¼" (6mm) in from the edge of the pocket (this will help reinforce the pocket, making it extra durable for even the most rough-and-tumble kid). Be sure to leave the top pocket flap free. Trim threads as needed.

9 Begin tag

Choose a particular design element from your fabric choice. Press fusible web to the back of the fabric, remove the paper backing and fuse a piece of batting on top of the web.

Roughly trim around the design with the batting.

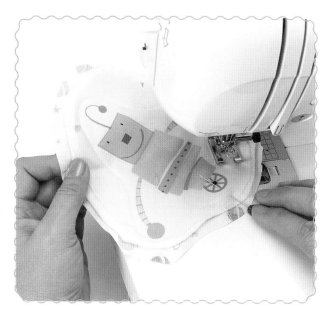

10 Add tag backing

Trim a piece of backing fabric approximately the same size as the front of the tag. Pin it to the tag, wrong sides together. Sew around the outside edge of the design.

Trim away excess fabric close to the stitching line. Stitch around the particular elements of the design, quilting the layers of fabric together.

TIP

If you have scallop edge scissor, use those to cut around the image; it will make a cute addition to the design.

11 Add buttons

Sew buttons to the four corners of the pocket flap (see Adding Buttons on page 32). Sew the top two buttons through all layers of the pocket and bag. Sew the bottom two buttons through the pocket flap fabric only. Fold the triangle down from the bottom edge of the pocket and sew a button to the center point of the triangle.

Sew a large button to the tote bag, just below the top edge of the pocket and close to the right-hand side of the bag.

12 Finish tote

Add a button to the inside of the pocket.

Attach a grommet to the top edge of the fabric tag. Follow the directions provided with the grommets. Attach the tag to the button just inside the pocket. The tag can hang on the inside or outside of the pocket.

Art To Go

Art can get messy, and sometimes it is necessary to travel to Art class. This cute duo of designs solves both problems, with artistic flair. What budding artist would not be thrilled to arrive to class totally prepared for anything and everything artsy?

materials

Natural canvas apron and tote bag

Fabric paint in black, white, green, grape and yellow

Paintbrushes in No. 0 liner, No. 5 round and No. 4 shader

1 yard (1m) gingham print fabric

Buttons

Black fabric marker

Measuring tape

Paper plate

Sewing machine

Iron

Straight pins

Needle

Thread

Materials for the following Techniques
• Garment Care and Handling (page 12)
• Creating and Transferring a Pattern (page 13)
• Painting on Fabric (page 15)
• Bias Tape (page 17)

Deconstruction

1 Prepare apron

Prepare the garment for use (see Garment Care and Handling on page 12).

Remove the stitching from the left shoulder seam of the apron. Take note of the measurement of one of the apron ties. Cut the ties from the sides of the apron and set aside.

Reconstruction

2 Make ties

Make 4 yards (3½m) of bias tape using the gingham fabric (see Bias Tape on page 17).

Cut four lengths of gingham bias tape the measurement of the ties you removed in step 1. Stitch the folded edge closed using a ¼" (6mm) seam allowance. These will be used as the apron ties.

3 Add binding to apron

Bind the top edge of the pocket. Using the straight pins, secure the bias tape over the edges of the apron (you will cover any original hems, seams and bindings of the apron). Pin the ties to the inside edge of the apron at the point where the ties were removed earlier.

4 Stitch on binding

Turn under the edges where the bias tape overlaps. Stitch through all the layers of bias tape and the apron.

5 Finish binding

Using straight pins, attach a length of bias tape to the neckline and stitch. Sew the shoulder seam closed following the original seam line.

6 Measure tote

Measure the circumference of the tote bag and cut a length of gingham bias tape this length plus 1" (3cm).

7 Attach binding

Press the bias tape open and pin it along the tote bag 1" (3cm) down from the top edge. Turn under the raw edges and stitch the top edge.

8 Overlap bias tape

When you come to the end of the bias tape, lay the loose end of the tape over the sewn end and stitch through the overlap.

Repeat steps 6 and 7 to secure the bottom edge of the bias tape.

9 Add bow

Using a 10" (25cm) section of bias tape pressed completely open, tie a two-loop bow. Trim the ends of the bow at an angle and fray the edges. Using a needle and thread, sew the bow to the front of the bag on top of the binding. If desired, embellish with a button.

10 Paint designs

Transfer the designs (see the CD) to the apron and tote bag fronts (see Creating and Transferring a Pattern on page 13).

Prepare the apron and tote for painting (see Painting on Fabric on page 15). Using the paints and the liner, round and shading paintbrushes, paint the designs following the project photo as a guide to color placement. Using the liner brush, add white highlights to the paint bottles. Let the paint dry thoroughly.

Outline the designs using the black fabric marker.

Follow the manufacturer's instructions to set the paint and the marker ink.

Retro Garden Apron

Gardening is extremely popular these days among people of all ages. Little helpers are always eager to get their hands dirty but perhaps not their clothing. Looking good while being good to the planet is a winning combination.

materials

Child's apron

Seam ripper

Measuring tape

¼ yard (¼m) fabric

Scissors

Iron

Sewing machine

¼" (6mm) wide elastic

Safety pin

Straight pins

Hook and loop tape

Fabric paint in colors that correspond to your fabric choice

Paintbrushes in No. 0 liner, No. 5 round and No. 4 shader

Cotton swab

Needle

Thread

Button

Materials for the following Techniques
- Creating and Transferring a Pattern (page 13)
- Painting on Fabric (page 15)

Deconstruction

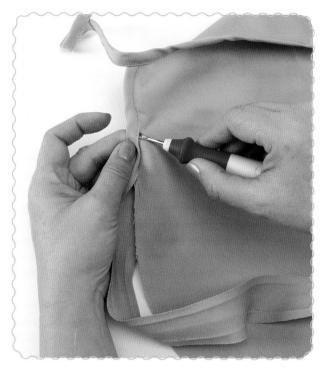

1 Partially remove binding
Measure down 3" (8cm) from each of the apron ties and remove the stitching using the seam ripper, freeing, but not removing, the binding from the sides and bottom edges of the apron.

Note

The remaining portion of the binding will still be attached to the apron.

Reconstruction

2 Prepare pocket
Measure across the front of the apron and double this measurement. Using this number, cut a piece of fabric × 8½" (22cm) wide. Turn under the top edge of the fabric ¼" (6mm) and press. Turn under an additional 1½" (4cm) and press again.

3 Create casing for pocket
Stitch ¾" (2cm) down from the top edge of the pocket and then again, ⅜" (9mm) down from the first row of stitching, forming a casing.

4 Sew gathering rows of stitching

Sew a row of gathering stitches ¼" (6mm) up from the bottom edge of the apron pocket.

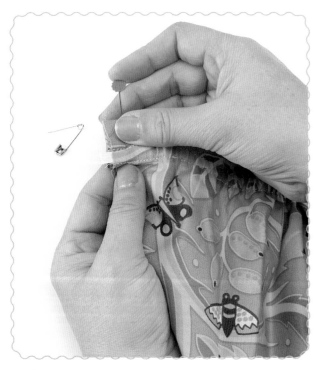

5 Add elastic to casing

Cut a length of elastic the width of the apron. Attach the safety pin to one end of the elastic. Thread the elastic through the casing. Pin each of the elastic ends to the edges of the pocket.

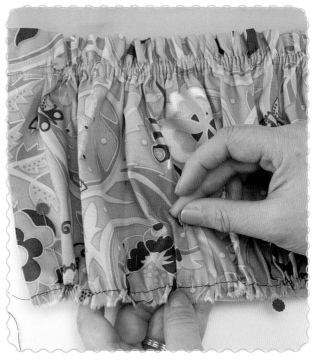

6 Secure pocket to apron

Place a pin at the center point along the bottom edge of the apron. Pin the apron pocket to the front of the apron, matching the center pins and the bottom edges of both the pocket and the apron. Adjust the gathers by pulling the gathering threads until the sides of the pocket meet the apron sides. Pin well.

Note

The curve of the apron hemline is not intended to match the straight edge of the pocket at this point. Allow the excess fabric from the pocket to drape past the curves of the apron hemline; it will be trimmed away after the stitching is complete.

7 Stitch pocket

Flip the apron over. Stitch across the sides and bottom edges of the apron, following the lines of the apron, to secure the pocket.

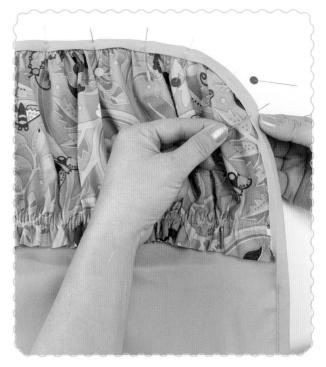

9 Pin binding

Turn the apron so the pocket is facing up. Pin the apron's original binding, encasing the pocket and apron between the layers of binding.

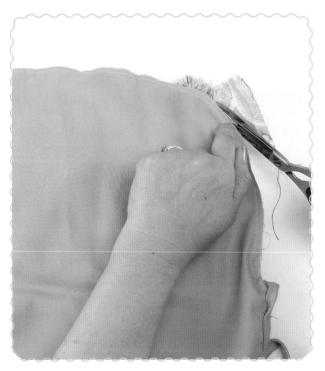

8 Trim excess fabric

Using the scissors, trim the excess pocket fabric evenly with the apron.

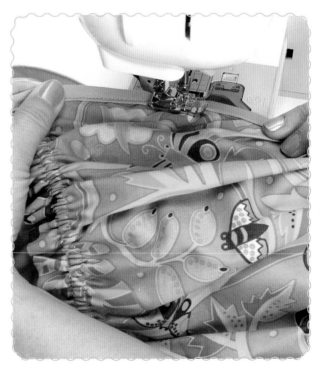

10 Stitch binding closed

Topstitch through all the layers of the fabric to reattach the binding.

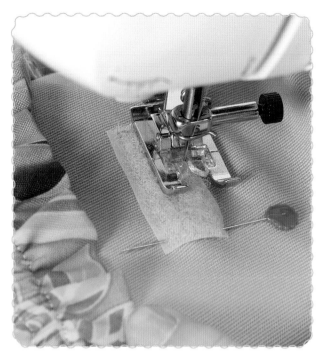

11 Add hook-and-loop tape

Position one side of a 2" (5cm) piece of hook-and-loop tape along the center top edge on the inside of the fabric pocket. Sew it into place. Sew the opposite side of the tape to the apron.

13 Add button

Repeat step 12 to paint the large flower. Let the paint dry. Refer to the paint manufacturer's directions to set the paint.

Using the needle and thread, sew a button to the center of the large flower.

12 Transfer pattern and paint design

Transfer the pattern provided (see the CD) or your own creation to the fabric (see Creating and Transferring a Pattern on page 13).

Prepare the apron and your surface for painting (see Painting on Fabric on page 15). Paint in the desired design elements, letting them dry between coats. Use the liner brush to add highlights, outline figures and add antennas, vein lines, etc. Use a cotton swab dipped into paint to create dots. Let the paints dry thoroughly.

Resources

I would like to thank the following companies for their support. You will recognize their wonderful products in the projects throughout the book. Their generosity has made the completion of this book all that more pleasurable.

Alexander Henry
- "mini monroe" The Alexandra Henry Collection© 2007

BagWorks Inc.
- Child's Smock Apron #0188-Natural
- Tote Bag-Natural
- Child's Apron #0146-Apple
- Sling Backpack #2390-Tangerine
- Mini Zip Backpack #0125-Natural
Fort Worth, Texas
www.bagworks.com

Beacon Adhesives
- Beacon 527 Multi-Use Glue, Fabri-Tac craft adhesives
125 MacQuesten Parkway S.
Mount Vernon, NY 10550
Phone: 914-699-3405
www.beaconcreates.com

Blumenthal Lansing Co.
- La Mode Buttons
1929 Main St.
Lansing, IA 52151
www.blumenthallansing.com

Clover Needlecraft Inc.
- Quick Yo-Yo Maker (Large)
- Sewing notions, cutting tools
13438 Alondra Blvd.
Cerritos, CA 90703
Phone: 800-233-1703
www.clover-usa.com

DecoArt
- Americana white nylon fabric painting brushes (No. 0 liner, No. 5 round, No. 4 shader, No. 6 shader)
- SoSoft Paint
Stanford, KY 40484
www.decoart.com

DMC
- Pearl cotton and embroidery floss
South Hackensack Ave.
Port Kearny Building 10F
South Kearney, NJ 07032
Phone: 973-589-0606
www.dmc-usa.com

Dritz
- Sew-On Snaps no.4
Prym Consumer USA
Spartanburg, SC 29304
www.dritz.com

Duncan Enterprises
- Tulip Express Yourself!
5673 E. Shields Ave.
Fresno, CA 93727
Phone: 800-438-6226
www.duncancrafts.com

Ellison
- Sizzix Bigz and Originals Dies & BIGkick diecut machine
- 654981 Daisies, 38-0224 Flower #1, 38-0227 Leaf / Stem, 654997 Sun #3
25862 Commercentre Drive
Lake Forest, CA 92630
Phone: 877-355-4766
www.Sizzix.com

Jesse James Company
- Dress It Up Natural Shell Shape Buttons, yellow #1535
- Dress It Up - Candy Cane
Bethlehem, PA
www.dressitup.com

Tools GS
- Fabric Cement
1150 University Ave., Suite 5
Rochester, NY 14607
Phone: 800-295-3050
www.ToolsGS.com

Uchida of America Corp.
- DecoColor Opaque Paint Markers
www.marvy.com

The Warm Company
- Fusible products, including Steam-a-Seam2
5529 186th Place, SW
Lynnwood, WA 98037
Phone: 425-248-2424
www.warmcompany.com

Wrights
- Baby Rick Rack blue
- single-fold bias tape
Antioch, TN 37013
www.wrights.com

Index

More easy sewing projects
can be found in these Krause Publications titles

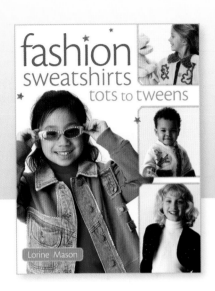

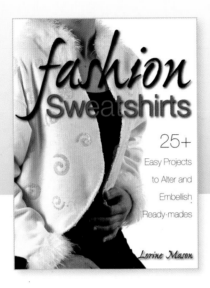

Fashion Sweatshirts: Tots to Tweens

by Lorine Mason

Turn a simple, inexpensive sweatshirt into a personal design statement. Your child will love the 20 adorable girl and boy designs for altering a simple sweatshirt into a fashion statement for tots to the more sophisticated pre-teens.

This book is also a resource guide for technique—a jumping off point for getting started in altered clothing, or a step-by-step guide to create your own version of a featured design.

ISBN 10: 0-89689-704-4
ISBN 13: 978-0-89689-704-5
128 pages / paperback / Z2405

Fashion Sweatshirts

by Lorine Mason

With *Fashion Sweatshirts* you'll learn how to use the latest techniques to turn a simple, inexpensive sweatshirt into a personal fashion statement with contemporary flair.

Featuring 29 sweatshirt projects focusing on women's designs as well as several designs for children, all using today's most popular fabrics and styles, this book offers you a unique, fun and inexpensive way to update your wardrobe.

ISBN 10: 0-87349-912-3
ISBN 13: 978-0-87349-912-5
128 pages / paperback / FSHSW

Low-Sew Boutique

by Cheryl Weiderspahn

Cheryl Weiderspahn shows you how to creatively use simple ready-made rugs, towels, potholders, ribbons and more to make over 20 fantastic accessories, including handbags, backpacks, a travel set, a winter ensemble and tote bags. It's fast. It's easy.

Low-Sew Boutique is perfect for the novice sewer looking to create innovative low-sew projects as well as the experienced sewer looking for a few sewing "short cuts."

ISBN 10: 0-89689-434-7
ISBN 13: 978-0-89689-434-1
128 pages / paperback / Z0378